Curious Punishments *of*
Bygone Days

The Drunkards Cloak.

PUBLICATION NO. 33: PATTERSON SMITH REPRINT SERIES IN CRIMINOLOGY, LAW ENFORCEMENT, AND SOCIAL PROBLEMS

Curious Punishments
of
Bygone Days,

by

Alice Morse Earle.

The Illustrations
BY FRANK HAZENPLUG

Montclair, New Jersey
PATTERSON SMITH
1969

Originally published 1896
Reprinted 1969 by
Patterson Smith Publishing Corporation
Montclair, New Jersey

SBN 87585-033-2

Library of Congress Catalog Card Number: 69-14922

The Contents

FOREWORD.

In ransacking old court records, newspapers, diaries and letters for the historic foundation of the books which I have written on colonial history, I have found and noted much of interest that has not been used or referred to in any of those books. An accumulation of notes on old-time laws, punishments and penalties has evoked this volume. The subject is not a pleasant one, though it often has a humorous element; but a punishment that is obsolete gains an interest and dignity from antiquity and its history becomes endurable because it has a past only and no future. That men were pilloried and women ducked by our law-abiding forbears rouses a thrill of hot indignation which dies down into a dull ember of curiosity when we reflect that they will never be pilloried or ducked again.

An old-time writer dedicated his book to "All curious and ingenious gentlemen and gentlewomen who can gain from acts of the past a delight in the present days of virtue, wisdom and the humanities." It does not detract from the good intent and complacency of these old words that the writer lived in the days when the pillory, stocks and whipping-post stood brutally rampant in every English village.

Now, we also boast that, as Pope says:

" Taught by time our hearts have learned to glow
For others' good, and melt for others' woe."

And I too dedicate this book to all curious and ingenious gentlemen and gentlewomen of our own days of virtue, wisdom and the humanities; and I trust any chance reader a century hence — if such reader there be — may in turn be not too harsh in judgment on an age that had to form powerful societies and associations to prevent cruelty — not to hardened and vicious criminals — but to faithful animals and innocent children.

Laying by
   the heels
      in the Bilboes.

Curious Punishments *of* Bygone Days

I

THE BILBOES

There is no doubt that our far-away grandfathers, whether of English, French, Dutch, Scotch or Irish blood, were much more afraid of ridicule than they were even of sinning, and far more than we are of extreme derision or mockery to-day. This fear and sensitiveness they showed in many ways. They were vastly touchy and resentful about being called opprobrious or bantering names ; often running petulantly to the court about it and seeking redress by prosecution of the offender. And they were forever bringing suits in petty slander and libel cases. Colonial court-rooms " bubbled over with scandal and gossip and spite." A creature as obsolete as his name, a " makebayt," was ever-present in the community, ever whispering slander, ever exciting contention, and often also haled to court for punishment ; while his opposite, a make-peace, was everywhere sadly needed. Far-seeing magistrates declared against the make-bait, as even guilty of stirring up bar- ratry, or as Judge Sewall, the old Boston Puritan termed it, at least "gravaminous."

Equally with personal libel did all good citizens and all good Christians fiercely resent of word, not only of derision or satire, but even of dispassionate disapproval of either government or church. A tithe of the plain- speaking criticism cheerfully endured in poli- tics to-day would have provoked a civil war two centuries ago ; while freedom of judgment or expression in religious matters was ever sharply silenced and punished in New England.

That ultra-sensativeness which made a lampoon, a jeer, a scoff, a taunt, an unbear- able and inflaming offence, was of equal force when used against the men of the day in punishment for real crimes and offenses.

In many — indeed, in nearly all — of the penalties and punishments of past centuries, derision, scoffing, contemptuous publicity and personal obloquy were applied to the offender or criminal by means of demeaning, degrading and helpless exposure in grotesque, insulting and painful "engines of punishment," such as the stocks, bilboes, pillory, brank, ducking-stool or jougs. Thus confined and exposed to the free gibes and constant mocking of the whole community, the peculiar power of the punishment was accented. Kindred in their nature and in their force were the punishments of setting on the gallows and of branding; the latter, whether in permanent form by searing the flesh, or by mutilation; or temporarily, by labeling with written placards or affixed initials.

One of the earliest of these degrading engines of confinement for public exposure, to be used in punishment in this country, was the bilboes. Though this instrument to "punyssche transgressours ageynste ye Kinges Maiesties lawes" came from old England, it was by tradition derived from Bilboa. It is alleged that bilboes were manufactured there and shipped on board the Spanish Armada in large numbers to shackle the English prisoners so confidently expected to be captured. This occasion may have given them their wide popularity and employment; but this happened in 1588, and in the first volume of *Hakluyt's Voyages*, page 295, dating some years earlier, reference is made to bilbous.

They were a simple but effective restraint; a long heavy bolt or bar of iron having two sliding shackles, something like handcuffs, and a lock. In these shackles were thrust the legs of offenders or criminals, who were then locked in with a padlock. Sometimes a chain at one end of the bilboes attached both bilboes and prisoner to the floor or wall; but this was superfluous, as the iron bar prevented locomotion. Whether the Spanish Armada story is true or not, bilboes were certainly much used on board ship. Shakespeare says in *Hamlet :* " Methought I lay worse than the mutines in the bilboes." In *Cook's Voyages* and other sea-tales we read of " bilboo-bolts " on sailors.

The Massachusetts magistrates brought bilboes from England as a means of punishing refractory or sinning colonists, and they were

4

soon in constant use. In the very oldest
court records, which are still preserved, of the
settlement of Boston—the Bay colony—
appear the frequent sentences of offenders to
be placed in the bilboes. The earliest entry
is in the authorized record of the Court held
at Boston on the 7th of August, 1632. It
reads thus: "Jams Woodward shall be sett
in the bilbowes for being drunk at the Newe-
towne." "Newe-towne" was the old name
of Cambridge. Soon another colonist felt
the bilboes for "selling peeces and powder
and shott to the Indians," ever a bitterly-
abhorred and fiercely-punished crime. And
another, the same year, for threatening —
were he punished — he would carry the case
to England, was summarily and fearlessly
thrust into the bilboes.

Then troublesome Thomas Dexter, with
his ever-ready tongue, was hauled up and tried
on March 4, 1633. Here is his sentence:

"Thomas Dexter shal be sett in the bilbowes, disfranchized, and fyned £15 for
speking rpchfull and seditious words agt the
government here established." He also suffered in the bilboes for cursing, for "pro-

phane saying dam ye come." Thomas Morton of Mare-Mount, that amusing old debauchee and roysterer, was sentenced to be "clapt into the bilbowes." And he says "the harmeles salvages" stared at him in wonder "like poore silly lambes" as he endured his punishment, and doubtless some of "the Indesses, gay lasses in beaver coats" who had danced with him around his merry Maypole and had partaken of his cask of "claret sparkling neat" sympathized with him and cheered him in his indignity.

The next year another Newe-towne man, being penitent, Henry Bright, was set in the bilboes for "swearynge." Another had "sleited the magistrates in speaches." In 1635, on April 7, Griffin Montagne "shal be sett in ye bilbowes for stealing boards and clapboards and enjoyned to move his habit-acon." Within a year we find offenders being punished in two places for the same offence, thus degrading them far and wide; and when in Salem they were "sett in the stockes," we find always in Boston that the bilboes claimed its own. Women suffered this punishment as well as men. Francis

Weston's wife and others were set in the bilboes.

It is high noon in Boston in the year 1638. The hot June sun beats down on the little town, the narrow paths, the wharfs; and the sweet-fern and cedars on the common give forth a pungent dry hot scent that is wafted down to the square where stands the Governor's house, the market, the church, the homes of the gentlefolk. A crowd is gathered there around some interesting object in the middle of the square; visitors from Newe-towne and Salem, Puritan women and children, tawny Indian braves in wampum and war-paint, gaily dressed sailors from two great ships lying at anchor in the bay — all staring and whispering, or jeering and biting the thumb. They are gathered around a Puritan soldier, garbed in trappings of military bravery, yet in but sorry plight. For it is training day in the Bay colony, and in spite of the long prayer with which the day's review began, or perhaps before that pious opening prayer, Serjeant John Evins has drunken too freely of old Sack or Alicant, and the hot sun and the sweet wine have sent him reeling from the ranks in disgrace. There he sits, sweltering in his great coat "basted with cotton-wool and thus made defensive ag't Indian arrowes;" weighed down with his tin armor, a heavy corselet covering his body, a stiff gorget guarding his throat, clumsy tasses protecting his thighs, all these "neatly varnished black," and costing twenty-four shillings apiece of the town's money. Over his shoulder hangs another weight, his bandelier, a strong "neat's leather" belt, carrying twelve boxes of solid cartridges and a well-filled bullet-bag; and over all and heavier than all hangs from his neck — as of lead — the great letter D. Still from his wrist dangles his wooden gun-rest, but his "bastard musket with a snaphance" lies with his pike degraded in the dust.

The serjeant does not move at the jeers of the sailors, nor turn away from the wondering stare of the savages — he cannot move, he cannot turn away, for his legs are firmly set in the strong iron bilboes which John Winthrop sternly brought from England to the new land. Poor John Evins! Your head aches from the fumes of the cloying sack, your legs ache from the bonds of the clogging bilboes, your body aches from the clamps of your trumpery armor, but you will have to sit there in distress and in obloquy till acerb old John Norton, the pious Puritan preacher, will come "to chide" you, as is his wont, to point out to your fellow-citizens and to visitors your sinful fall, the disgracing bilboes, and the great letter that brands you as a drunkard.

The decade of life of the Boston bilboes was soon to end, it was to be " laid flat," as Sir Matthew Hale would say ; a rival entered the field. In 1639 Edward Palmer made for Boston with " planks and woodwork," a pair of stocks.

Planks and woodwork were plentiful everywhere in the new world, and iron and iron-workers at first equally scarce; so stocks soon were seen in every town, and the bilboes were disused, sold perhaps for old iron, wherein they again did good service. In Virginia the bilboes had a short term of use in the earliest years of the settlement ; the Provost-marshal had a fee of ten shillings for " laying by the heels ; '' and he was fre-

quently employed; but there, also, stocks
and pillory proved easier of construction and
attainment.

I would not be over-severe upon the bilboes in their special use in those early colonial settlements. There had to be some
means of restraint of vicious and lawless folk,
of hindering public nuisances, and a prison
could not be built in a day; the bilboes
seemed an easy settlement of the difficulty,
doing effectually with one iron bar what a
prison cell does with many. It was not their
use, but their glare of publicity that was
offensive. They were ever placed on offenders
in the marketplace, in front of the meeting
house on lecture day, on market day; not to
keep prisoners in lonely captivity but in public obloquy; and as has here been cited, for
what appear to us to-day slight offenses.

The Ducking-Stool

II

THE DUCKING STOOL

The ducking stool seems to have been placed on the lowest and most contempt-bearing stage among English instruments of punishment. The pillory and stocks, the gibbet, and even the whipping-post, have seen many a noble victim, many a martyr. But I cannot think any save the most ignoble criminals ever sat in a ducking-stool. In all the degrading and cruel indignities offered the many political and religious offenders in England under the varying rules of both church and state, through the fifteenth, sixteenth and seventeenth centuries, the ducking-stool played no part and secured no victims. It was an engine of punishment specially assigned to scolding women; though sometimes kindred offenders, such as slanderers, "makebayts," "chyderers," brawlers, railers, and women of light carriage also suffered through it. Though gruff old Sam

Johnson said to a gentle Quaker lady: " Madam, we have different modes of restraining evil — stocks for men, a ducking-stool for women, and a pound for beasts;" yet men as well as women-scolds were punished by being set in the ducking-stool, and quarrelsome married couples were ducked, tied back-to-back. The last person set in the Rugby ducking-stool was a brutal husband who had beaten his wife. Brewers of bad beer and bakers of bad bread were deemed of sufficiently degraded ethical standing to be ducked. Unruly paupers also were thus subdued.

That intelligent French traveler, Misson, who visited England about the year 1700, and who left in his story of his travels so much valuable and interesting information of the England of that day, gives this lucid description of a ducking-stool:

" The way of punishing scolding women is pleasant enough. [They fasten an armchair to the end of two beams twelve or fifteen feet long, and parallel to each other, so that these two pieces of wood with their two ends embrace the chair, which hangs between them by a sort of axle, by which means it plays freely, and always remains in the natural horizontal position in which a chair should be, that a person may sit conveniently in it, whether you raise it or let it down. They set up a post on the bank of a pond or river, and over this post they lay, almost in equilibrio, the two pieces of wood, at one end of which the chair hangs just over the water. They place the woman in this chair and so plunge her into the water as often as the sentence directs, in order to cool her immoderate heat."

The adjectives pleasant and convenient as applied to a ducking-stool would scarcely have entered the mind of any one but a Frenchman. Still the chair itself was sometimes rudely ornamented. The Cambridge stool was carved with devils laying hold of scolds. Others were painted with appropriate devices such as a man and woman scolding. Two Plymouth ducking-stools still preserved are of wrought iron of good design. The Sandwich ducking-stool bore the motto:

" Of members ye tonge is worst or beste
An yll tonge oft doth breede unreste."

We read in Blackstone's *Commentaries:*

" A common scold may be indicted, and if convicted shall be sentenced to be placed in a certain engine of correction called the tre-bucket, castigatory, or ducking-stool."

The trebuchet, or trebucket, was a sta-tionary and simple form of a ducking machine consisting of a short post set at the water's edge with a long beam resting on it like a see-saw; by a simple contrivance it could be swung round parallel to the bank, and the culprit tied in the chair affixed to one end. Then she could be swung out over the water and see-sawed up and down into the water. When this machine was not in use, it was secured to a stump or bolt in the ground by a padlock, because when left free it proved too tempting and convenient an opportunity for tormenting village children to duck each other.

A tumbrel, or scold's-cart, was a chair set on wheels and having very long wagon-shafts, with a rope attached to them about two feet from the end. When used it was wheeled into a pond backward, the long shafts were suddenly tilted up, and the scold sent down in a backward plunge into the water. When the ducking was accomplished, the tumbrel was drawn out of the water by the ropes. Collinson says in his *History of Somersetshire*, written in 1791: "In Shipton Mallet was anciently set up a tumbrel for the correction of unquiet women." Other names for a like engine were gumstool and coqueen-stool.

·Many and manifold are the allusions to the ducking-stool in English literature. In a volume called *Miscellaneous Poems*, written by Benjamin West and published in 1780, is a descriptive poem entitled *The Ducking-stool*, which runs thus:

> " There stands, my friend, in yonder pool
> An engine called the ducking-stool;
> By legal power commanded down
> The joy and terror of the town.
> If jarring females kindle strife,
> Give language foul, or lug the coif,
> If noisy dames should once begin
> To drive the house with horrid din,
> Away, you cry, you'll grace the stool;
> We'll teach you how your tongue to rule.
> The fair offender fills the seat
> In sullen pomp, profoundly great;
> Down in the deep the stool descends,
> But here, at first, we miss our ends;

She mounts again and rages more
Than ever vixen did before.
So, throwing water on the fire
Will make it but burn up the higher.
If so, my friend, pray let her take
A second turn into the lake,
And, rather than your patience lose,
Thrice and again repeat the dose.
No brawling wives, no furious wenches,
No fire so hot but water quenches.''

In Scotland " flyting queans " sat in ignominy in cucking-stools. Bessie Spens was admonished : " Gif she be found flyteing with any neighbour, man or wife, and specially gains Jonet Arthe, she shall be put on the cuck-stule and sit there twenty-four hours." A worthless fellow, Sande Hay, " for troublance made upon Andro Watson, is discernit for his demerits to be put in the cuck-stule, there to remain till four hours after noon." The length of time of punishment — usually twenty-four hours — would plainly show there was no attendant ducking; and this cuck-stool, or cucking-stool, must not be confounded with the ducking-stool, which dates to the days of Edward the Confessor. The cuck-stool was simply a strong chair in which an offender was fastened, thus to be hooted at or pelted at by the mob. Sometimes, when placed on a tumbrel, it was used for ducking.

At the time of the colonization of America the ducking-stool was at the height of its English reign ; and apparently the amiability of the lower classes was equally at ebb. The colonists brought their tempers to the new land, and they brought their ducking-stools. Many minor and some great historians of this country have called the ducking-stool a Puritan punishment. I have never found in the hundreds of pages of court records that I have examined a single entry of an execution of ducking in any Puritan community; while in the " cavalier colonies," so called, in Virginia and the Carolinas, and in Quaker Pennsylvania, many duckings took place, and in law survived as long as similar punishments in England.

In the Statute Books of Virginia from Dale's time onward many laws may be found designed to silence idle tongues by ducking. One reads :

" Whereas oftentimes many brabling women often slander and scandalize their neighbours, for which their poore husbands are often brought into chargeable and vexatious suits and cast in great damages, be it enacted that all women found guilty be sentenced to ducking."

Others dated 1662 are most explicit.

" The court in every county shall cause to be set up near a Court House a Pillory, a pair of Stocks, a Whipping Post and a Ducking-Stool in such place as they think convenient, which not being set up within six month after the date of this act the said Court shall be fined 5,000 lbs. of tobacco.

" In actions of slander caused by a man's wife, after judgment past for damages, the woman shall be punished by Ducking, and if the slander be such as the damages shall be adjudged as above 500 lbs. of Tobacco, then the woman shall have ducking for every 500 lbs. of Tobacco adjudged against the husband if he refuse to pay the Tobacco."

The fee of a sheriff or constable for ducking was twenty pounds of tobacco.

The American Historical Record, Vol. I, gives a letter said to have been written to Governor Endicott, of Massachusetts, in

1634, by one Thomas Hartley, from Hungars Parish, Virginia. It gives a graphic description of a ducking-stool, and an account of a ducking in Virginia. I quote from it:

"The day afore yesterday at two of ye clock in ye afternoon I saw this punishment given to one Betsey wife of John Tucker who by ye violence of her tongue has made his house and ye neighborhood uncomfortable. She was taken to ye pond near where I am sojourning by ye officer who was joined by ye Magistrate and ye Minister Mr. Cotton who had frequently admonished her and a large number of People. They had a machine for ye purpose yt belongs to ye Parish, and which I was so told had been so used three times this Summer. It is a platform with 4 small rollers or wheels and two upright posts between which works a Lever by a Rope fastened to its shorter or heavier end. At ye end of ye longer arm is fixed a stool upon which sd Betsey was fastened by cords, her gown tied fast around her feete. The Machine was then moved up to ye edge of ye pond, ye Rope was slackened by ye officer and ye woman was allowed to go down under ye

water for ye space of half a minute. Betsey
had a stout stomach, and would not yield
until she had allowed herself to be ducked 5
several times. At length she cried piteously,
Let me go Let me go, by God's help I 'll sin
no more. Then they drew back ye Machine,
untied ye Ropes and let her walk home in
her wetted clothes a hopefully penitent
woman."

Bishop Meade, in his *Old Churches, Ministers and Families of Virginia*, tells of a "scolding quean" who was ordered to be ducked
three times from the yard arm of a vessel
lying in James Rver. A woman in North-
ampton County, Virginia, suffered a peculiarly
degrading punishment for slander. In the lack
of a ducking-stool she was " drawn ouer the
Kings Creeke at the starne of a boate or
Canoux, also the next Saboth day in the time
of diuine seruise " was obliged to present herself before the minister and congregation, and
acknowledge her fault and beg forgiveness.
From the *Decisions of Virginia General Court*
now being printed by the Virginia Historical
Society, we learn of one Margaret Jones that
at a court held at "James-Citty" on the 12th

of October, 1626 : " for ye severall offences
aforenamed, of ye said Margaret Jones, yt Shee
bee toughed or dragged at a boats Starne in ye
River from ye shoare unto the Margaret &
John and thence unto the shoare againe."

Toughed would seem a truly appropriate
word for this ordeal.   The provost marshal's
fees decreed by this court at this time were
ten shillings "for punishing any *man* by
ducking."

In 1634 two women were sentenced to be
either drawn from King's Creek " from one
Cowpen to another at the starn of a boat or
kanew," or to present themselves before the
congregation and ask public forgiveness of
each other and God.

In 1633 it was ordered that a ducking-
stool be built in every county in Maryland,
but I have no proof that they were ever built
or used, though it is probable they were.   At
a court-baron at St. Clements, the county
was prosecuted for not having one of these
"public conveniences."

Half a century elapsed after the settlement
of Massachusetts ere that commonwealth
ordered a ducking-stool.   On the 15th of

May, 1672, while Richard Bellingham was Governor, the court at Massachusetts Bay passed this law :

" Whereas there is no expresse punishment by any law hitherto established affixed to the evill practise of sundry persons by exorbitancy of the tonge in rayling and scolding, it is therefore ordered, that all such persons convicted, before any Court or magistrate that hath propper cognizance of the cause for rayling or scolding, shalbe gagged or sett in a ducking stoole & dipt ouer head & eares three times in some convenient place of fresh or salt water as the Court or magistrate shall judge meete."

Governor Bellingham's sister was a notorious scold, who suffered death as a witch.

John Dunton, writing from Boston in 1686, does not note the presence of a ducking-stool, but says :

" Scolds they gag and set them at their own Doors for certain hours together, for all comers and goers to gaze at ; were this a Law in England and well executed it wou'd in a little Time prove an Effectual Remedy to cure the Noise that is in many Women's heads."

22

This was a law well-executed at the time in Scotland, though Dunton was ignorant of it.

There are no entries to show that the law authorizing ducking ever was executed in Massachusetts nor in Maine, where a dozen towns — Kittery, York and others — were fined for "having no coucking-stool." It was ordered on Long Island that every Court of Sessions should have a ducking-stool; but nothing exists in their records to prove that the order was ever executed, or any Long Island woman ducked; nor is there proof that there was in New York city a ducking-stool, though orders were issued for one; a Lutheran minister of that city excused himself for striking a woman who angered him by her " scholding " because she was not punished by law therefor.

Pennsylvania, mild with the thees and thous of non-belligerent Quakers, did not escape scolding women. In 1708 the Common Council of Philadelphia ordered a ducking-stool to be built. In 1718 it was still lacking, and still desired, and still necessary. ´ "Whereas it has been frequently and often presented by several former Grand Jurys for this City the Necessity of a Ducking-stool and house of Correction for the just punishment of scolding Drunken Women, as well as divers other profligate and Unruly persons in this Town who are become a Publick Nuisance and disturbance to the Town in Generall, Therefore we the present Grand Jury Do Earnestly again present the same to the Court of Quarter Sessions for the City Desireing their Immediate Care That these Public Conveniances may not be any Longer Delay'd but with all possible Speed provided for the Detention and Quieting such Disorderly Persons."

For several years later the magistrates clamored for a ducking-stool, and the following indictment was brought against an unruly woman:

"City of Philadelphia. We the grand Inquest for our Lord the King upon respective oaths and affirmations Do present that Mary wife of John Austin late of Philadelphia, Cordwainer, the twenty-ninth day of September and divers other days and times as well before as after in the High City Ward in the

City afforsd within the Jurisdiction of this Court was and yet is a Common Scold, And the Peace of our Lord the King a common and publick Disturber, And Strife and Debate among her neighbours a Comon Sower and Mover, To the Great Disburbance of the Leige Subjects of our sd Lord the King Inhabiting the City afforsd, And to the Evill Example of other Such Cases & Delinquents And also agt the Peace of our Lord the King his Crown and Dignity."

As late as 1824 a Philadelphia scold was sentenced by this same Court of Sessions to be ducked; but the punishment was not inflicted, as it was deemed obsolete and contrary to the spirit of the time.

In 1777 a ducking-school was ordered at the confluence of the Ohio and Monongahela rivers — and doubtless it was erected and used.

In the year 1811, at the Supreme Court at Milledgeville, Georgia, one "Miss Palmer," who, the account says, "seems to have been rather glib on the tongue," was indicted, tried, convicted and punished for scolding, by being publicly ducked in the Oconee River. The editor adds : " Numerous spectators attended the execution of the sentence." Eight years later the Grand Jury of Burke County, of the same state, presented Mary Cammell as a "common scold and disturber of the peaceable inhabitants of the County." The *Augusta Chronicle* says this of the indictment:

" We do not know the *penalty*, or if there be any, attached to the offense of *scolding ;* but for the information of our Burke neighbours we would inform them that the late lamented and distinguished Judge Early decided, some years since, when a modern Xantippe was brought before him, that she should undergo the *punishment of lustration* by immersion three several times in the *Oconee*. Accordingly she was confined to the tail of a cart, and, accompanied by the hooting of a mob, conducted to the river, where she was publicly ducked, in conformity with the sentence of the court. Should this punishment be accorded Mary Cammell, we hope, however, it may be attended with a more salutary effect than in the case we have just alluded to — the unruly subject of which, each time as she rose from the watery element, impiously exclaimed, with a ludicrous gravity of countenance, 'Glory to God.'"

It is doubtful whether these Georgia duckings were done with a regularly constructed ducking-stool; the cart was probably run down into the water.

One of the latest, and certainly the most notorious sentences to ducking was that of Mrs. Anne Royal, of Washington, D. C., almost in our own day. This extraordinary woman had lived through an eventful career in love and adventure; she had been stolen by the Indians when a child, and kept by them fifteen years; then she was married to Captain Royall, and taught to read and write. She traveled much, and wrote several vituperatively amusing books. She settled down upon Washington society as editor of a newspaper called the "Washington Paul Pry'" and of another, the "Huntress"; and she soon terrorized the place. No one in public office was spared, either in personal or printed abuse, if any offense or neglect was given to her. A persistent lobbyist, she was shunned like the plague by all congressmen. John Quincy Adams called her an itinerant virago. She was arraigned as a common scold before Judge William Cranch, and he sentenced her to be ducked in the Potomac River. She was, however, released with a fine, and appears to us to-day to have been insane — possibly through over-humored temper.

The Stocks.

III

THE STOCKS

One of the earliest institutions in every New England community was a pair of stocks. The first public building was a meeting-house, but often before any house of God was builded, the devil got his restraining engine. It was a true English punishment, and to a degree, a Scotch; and was of most ancient date. In the *Cambridge Trinity College Psalter*, an illuminated manuscript illustrating the manners of the twelfth century, may be seen the quaint pictures of two men sitting in stocks, while two others flout them. So essential to due order and government were the stocks that every village had them. Sometimes they were movable and often were kept in the church porch, a sober Sunday monitor. Shakespeare says in King Lear:

> " Fetch forth the stocks
> You stubborn ancient knave!''

In England, petty thieves, unruly servants, wife-beaters, hedge-tearers, vagrants, Sabbath-breakers, revilers, gamblers, drunkards, ballad-singers, fortune-tellers, traveling musicians and a variety of other offenders, were all punished by the stocks. Doubtless the most notable person ever set in the stocks for drinking too freely was that great man, Cardinal Wolsey. About the year 1500 he was the incumbent at Lymington, and getting drunk at a village feast, he was seen by Sir Amyas Poulett, a strict moralist, and local justice of the peace, who humiliated the embryo cardinal by thrusting him in the stocks.

The Boston magistrates had a "pair of bilbowes" doubtless brought from England; but these were only temporary, and soon stocks were ordered. It is a fair example of the humorous side of Puritan law so frequently and unwittingly displayed that the first malefactor set in these strong new stocks was the carpenter who made them:

"Edward Palmer for his extortion in taking £1, 13s., 7d. for the plank and woodwork of Boston stocks is fyned £5 & censured to bee sett an houre in the stocks."

Thus did our ancestors make the "punishment fit the crime." It certainly was rather a steep charge, for Carpenter Robert Bartlett of New London made not long after "a pair of stocks with nine holes fitted for the irons," and only charged thirteen shillings and fourpence for his work. The carpenter of Shrewsbury, Massachusetts, likewise, as Pepys said of a new pair of stocks in his neighborhood, took handsel of the stocks of his own making.

In Virginia a somewhat kindred case was that of one Mr. Henry Charlton of Hungar's Parish in 1633. For slandering the minister, Mr. Cotton, Charlton was ordered "to make a pair of stocks and set in them several Sabbath days after divine service, and then ask Mr. Cotton's forgiveness for using offensive words concerning him."

In Maryland in 1655 another case may be cited. One William Bramhall having been convicted of signing a rebellious petition, was for a second offense of like nature ordered to be "at the Charge of Building a Pair of Stocks and see it finished within one Month." There is no reference to his punishment through the stocks of his own manufacture.

With a regard for the comfort of the criminal strangely at variance with what Cotton Mather termed "the Gust of the Age," and a profound submission to New England climate, a Massachusetts law; enacted June 18, 1645, declares that "he yt offens in excessive and longe drinkinge, he shalbe sett in the stocks for three howers *when the weather is seasonable*."

Just as soon as the Boston stocks had been well warmed by Carpenter Palmer they promptly started on a well-filled career of usefulness. They gathered in James Luxford, who had been "psented for having two wifes." He had to pay a fine of £100 and be set in the stocks one hour upon the following market-day after lecture, and on the next lecture-day also, where he could be plainly seen by every maid and widow in the little town, that there might be no wife Number Three. Then a watchman of the town, "for drinking several times of strong waters," took his turn. Soon a man for "uncivil carriages" was "stocked."

Every town was enjoined to build stocks. In 1655 Medfield had stocks, and in 1638 Newbury and Concord were fined for "the want of stocks," and Newbury was given time till the next court session to build them. The town obeyed the order, and soon John Perry was set in them for his "abusive carriage to his wife and child." Dedham and Watertown were "psent'd" in 1639 for "the want of stocks." Ipswich already had them, for John Wedgwood that same year was set in the stocks simply for being in the company of drunkards. In Yarmouth, a thief who stole flax and yarn, and in Rehoboth, one who stole an Indian child, were "stocked." Portsmouth, New Hampshire, built stocks and a cage. Plymouth had a constant relay of Quakers to keep her stocks from ever lying idle, as well as other offenders, such as Ann Savory, of unsavory memory. Rhode Island ordered "good sufficient stocks" in every town. In the southern and central colonies the stocks were a constant force. The Dutch favored the pillory and whipping-post, but a few towns had stocks. We find the Heer officer in Beverwyck (Albany) dispensing jus-

tice in a most summary manner. When
Martin de Metslaer wounded another in a
drunken brawl, the authorities hunted Martin
up, " early hauled him out of bed and set him
in the stocks." Connecticut was a firm advo-
cate of the stocks, and plentiful examples
might be given under New Haven and Connecticut laws.

Web Adey, who was evidently a " single-
man," for " two breaches of the Saboth " was
ordered to be set in the stocks, then to find a
master, and if not complying with this second
order the town would find one for him and
sell him for a term of service. This was the
arbitrary and not unusual method of disposing
of lazy, lawless and even lonely men, as well
as of more hardened criminals, who, when
sold for a term of service, usually got into
fresh disgrace and punishment through disobedience, idleness and running away.

I do not find many sentences of women to
be set in the stocks. Jane Boulton of Plymouth was stocked for reviling the magistrates; one of her neighbors sat in the
stocks and watched her husband take a flogging. Goody Gregory of Springfield in

1640, being grievously angered by a neighbor, profanely abused her, saying "Before God I could break thy head." She acknowledged her "great sine and fault" like a woman, but she paid her fine and sat in the stocks like a man, since she swore like one.

And it should be noted that the stocks were not for the punishment of *gentlemen*, they were thoroughly plebeian. The pillory was aristocratic in comparison, as was also branding with a hot iron.

Fiercely hedged around was divine worship. The stocks added their restraint by threatened use. "All persons who stand out of the meeting-house during time of service, to be set in the stocks."

In Plymouth in 1665 "all persons being without the dores att the meeting house on the Lords daies in houres of exercise, demeaneing themselves by jesting, sleeping, and the like, if they shall psist in such practices hee (the tithing-man) shall sett them in the stocks."

Regard for church and state were often combined by making public confession of sin in church with punishment in front of the church after the service. This was simply a carrying out of English customs. Mr. Hamilton, author of that interesting book, *Quarter Sessions from Queen Elizabeth to Queen Anne*, says, dealing with Devonshire :

" A favorite punishment for small offenses, such as resisting the constable, was the stocks. The offender had to come into the church at morning prayer, and say publicly that he was sorry; he was then set in the stocks until the end of the evening prayer. The punishment was generally repeated on the next market-day."

It seems scarcely necessary to describe the shape and appearance of stocks, for pictures of them are so common. They were formed by two heavy timbers the upper one of which could be raised, and when lowered, was held in place by a lock. In these two timbers were cut two half-circle notches which met two similar notches when the upper timber was in place and thus formed round holes, holding firmly in place the legs of the imprisoned culprit; sometimes the arms were thrust into smaller holes similarly formed. Usually, however, the culprit sat on a low bench with simply his legs confined. Thus securely restrained, he was powerless to escape the jests and jeers of every idler in the community.

The stocks were the scene of many striking figures, and many amusing ones; what a sight was that when an English actor who had caused the playing of the Midsummer-Night's Dream in the very house of the Bishop of Lincoln, and on Sunday, too, was set in stocks at the Bishop's gate with an ass's head beside him and a wisp of hay — in derision of the part he had played, that of Bottom the weaver. This in 1631 — after both Plymouth and Boston had been settled.

And the stocks were not without their farcical side in New England. Governor Winthrop's account of the exploits of a Boston Dogberry in 1644 is certainly amusing.

" There fell out a troublesome business in Boston. An English sailor happened to be drunk, and was carried to his lodging, and the constable (a godly man and much zealous against such disorders), hearing of it, found him out, being upon his bed asleep, so he awaked him, and led him to the stocks, no magistrate being at home. He being in the stocks, one of La Tour's French gentlemen visitors in Boston lifted up the stocks and let him out. The constable, hearing of it, went to the Frenchman (being then gone and quiet) and would needs carry *him* to the stocks. The Frenchman offered to yield himself to go to prison, but the constable, not understanding his language pressed him to go to the stocks : the Frenchman resisted and drew his sword; with that company came in and disarmed him, and carried him by force to the stocks, but soon after the constable took him out and carried him to prison, and presently after, took him forth again, and delivered him to La Tour. Much tumult was there about this : many Frenchmen were in town, and other strangers, who were not satisfied with this dealing of the constable yet were quiet. In the morning the magistrate examined the cause, and sent for La Tour, who was much grieved for his servant's miscarriage, and also for the disgrace put upon him (for in France it is a most ignominious thing to be laid in the stocks), but yet he complained not of any injury, but left him wholly with the magistrates to do with him what they pleased, etc.   .   .   .

The constable was the occasion of all this transgressing the bounds of his office, and that in six things.   1. In fetching a man out of his lodging that was asleep upon his bed, and without any warrant from authority.   2. In not putting a hook upon the stocks, nor setting some to guard them.   3. In laying hands upon the Frenchman that had opened the stocks when he was gone and quiet.   4. In carrying him to prison without warrant. 5. In delivering him out of prison without warrant.   6. In putting such a reproach upon a stranger and a gentleman when there was no need, for he knew he would be forthcoming and the magistrate would be at home that evening; but such are the fruits of ignorant and misguided zeal.   .   .   .   .   But the magistrates thought not convenient to lay these things to the constable's charge before the assembly, but rather to admonish him for it in private, lest they should have discouraged and discountenanced an honest officer."

Truly this is a striking and picturesque scene in colonial life, one worthy of Hogarth's pencil. The bronzed English sailor, inflamed with drink, ear-ringed, pigtailed, with short, wide, flapping trousers and brave with sash and shining cutlass; the gay, volatile French-man, in the beautiful and courtly dress of his day and nation, all laces and falbalas; and the solemn pragmatic Puritan tipstaff, with long wand of black and white, and horn lanthorn, with close-cropped head, sad-colored in garments, severe of feature, zealous in duty; and the spectators standing staring at the stocks; Indian stragglers, fair Puritan maidens, fierce sailor-men, a pious preacher or sober magistrate — no lack of local color in that picture.

It is interesting to note in all the colonies the attempt to exterminate all idle folk and idle ways. The severity of the penalties were so salutary in effect, that as Mrs. Good-win says in her *Colonial Cavalier*, they soon would have exterminated even that social pest, the modern tramp. Vagrants, and those who were styled "transients," were fiercely ab-horred and cruelly spurned. I have found by comparison of town records that they were often whipped from town to town, only to be thrust forth in a few weeks with fresh stripes to another grudged resting place. Such entries as this of the town of Westerly, Rhode Island, might be produced in scores:

"September 26, 1748. That the officer shall take the said transient forthwith to some publick place in this town and strip him from the waist upward, & whyp him twenty strypes well layd on his naked back, and then be by said officer transported out of this town."

The appearance of crime likewise had to be avoided. In 1635 Thomas Petet "for suspition of slander, idleness and stubbornness is to be severely whipt and kept in hold."

More shocking and still more summary was the punishment meted out to a Frenchman who was *suspected* only of setting fire to Boston in the year 1679. He was ordered to stand in the pillory, have both ears cut off, pay the charges of the court, and lie in prison in bonds of five hundred pounds until sentence was performed.

These Massachusetts magistrates were not the only ones to sentence punishment on suspicion. In Scotland one Richardson, a tailor, being "accusit of pickrie," or pilfering, was

adjudged to be punished with " twelve straiks
with ane double belt, because there could be
nae sufficient proof gotten, but vehement
suspition."

Writing of punishments of bygone days,
an English rhymester says :

" Each mode has served its turn, and played a part
    For good or ill with man ; but while the bane
Of drunkenness corrupts the nation's heart —
    Discrediting our age — methinks the reign
Of stocks, at least, were well revived again."

There is, in truth, a certain fitness in setting in the stocks for drunkenness ; a firm
confining of the wandering uncertain legs ; a
fixing in one spot for quiet growing sober,
and meditating on the misery of drunkenness,
a fitness that with the extreme of publicity
removed, or the wantonness of the spectators
curbed, perhaps would not be so bad a restraining punishment after all. Some of the great-
ness and self-control of the later years of Cardinal Wolsey's life may have come from those
hours of mortification and meditation spent in
the stocks. And over the stocks might be
set " a paper " as of yore, bearing in capital
letters the old epitaph found in solemn warn-

ing of eternity on many an ancient tomb-
stone but literally applicable in this temporal
matter.

> " All Ye who see the State of Me
> Think of the Glass that Runs for Thee."

IV

THE PILLORY.

Hawthorne says in his immortal *Scarlet Letter :*

" This scaffold constituted a portion of a penal machine which now, for two or three generations past, has been merely historical or traditionary among us, but was held in the old time to be as effectual in the promotion of good citizenship as ever was the guillotine among the terrorists of France. It was, in short, the platform of the pillory ; and above it rose the framework of that instrument of discipline, so fashioned as to confine the human head in its tight grasp, and thus hold it up to the public gaze. The very ideal of ignominy was embodied and made manifest in this contrivance of wood and iron. There can be no outrage, methinks — against our common nature — whatever be the delinquencies of the individual — no outrage more

The Pillory.

flagrant than to forbid the culprit to hide his face for shame."

This " essence of punishment " — the pillory or stretch-neck — can be traced back to a remote period in England and on the Continent— certainly to the twelfth century. In its history, tragedy and comedy are equally blended; and martyrdom and obloquy are alike combined. Seen in a prominent position in every village and town, its familiarity of presence was its only retrieving characteristic ; near church-yard and in public square was it ever found; local authorities forfeited the right to hold a market unless they had a pillory ready for use.

A description of a pillory is not necessary to one who has read any illustrated history of the English Church, of the Quakers, Dissenters, or of the English people; for the rude prints of political and religious sufferers in the pillory have been often reproduced. Douce, in his *Illustrations of Shakespeare* gives six different forms of the pillory. It was an upright board, hinged or divisible in twain, with a hole in which the head was set fast, and usually with two openings also for the hands. Often the ears were nailed to the wood on either side of the head-hole. Examples exist of a small finger-pillory or thumb-stocks, but are rare.

It would be impossible to enumerate the offences for which Englishmen were pilloried : among them were treason, sedition, arson, blasphemy, witch-craft, perjury, wife-beating, cheating, forestalling, forging, coin-clipping, tree-polling, gaming, dice-cogging, quarrelling, lying, libelling, slandering, threatening, conjuring, fortune-telling, "prigging," drunkenness, impudence. One man was set in the pillory for delivering false dinner invitations ; another for a rough practical joke ; another for selling an injurious quack medicine. All sharpers, beggars, impostors, vagabonds, were liable to be pilloried. So fierce sometimes was the attack of the populace with various annoying and heavy missiles on pilloried prisoners that several deaths are known to have ensued. On the other side, it is told in Chamber's *Book of Days* that a prisoner, by the sudden collapse of a rotten foot-board, was left hanging by his neck in danger of his life. On being liberated he brought action against the town and received damages.

The pillory in England has seen many a noble victim. The history of Puritanism, of Reformation, is filled with hundreds of pages of accounts of sufferings on the pillory. When such names as those of Leighton, Prynne, Lilburne, Burton and Bastwick appear as thus being punished we do not think of the pillory as a scaffold for felons, but as a platform for heroes. Who can read unmoved that painful, that pathetic account of the punishment of Dr. Bastwick. His weeping wife stood on a stool and kissed his poor pilloried face, and when his ears were cut off she placed them in a clean handkerchief and took them away, with emotions unspeakable and undying love.

De Foe said, in his famous *Hymn to the Pillory*:

" Tell us, great engine, how to understand
   Or reconcile the justice of this land ;
   How Bastwick, Prynne, Hunt, Hollingsby and
      Pye —
   Men of unspotted honesty —
   Men that had learning, wit and sense,
   And more than most men have had since,

Could equal title to thee claim
With Oates and Fuller, men of fouler fame.''

Lecture-day, as affording in New England, in the pious community, the largest gathering of reproving spectators, was the day chosen in preference for the performance of public punishment by the pillory. Hawthorne says of the Thursday Lecture : " The tokens of its observance are of a questionable cast. It is in one sense a day of public shame; the day on which transgressors who have made themselves liable to the minor severities of the Puritan law receive their reward of ignominy." Thus Nicholas Olmstead, in in Connecticut, is to " stand on the pillory at Hartford the next lecture-day." He was to be " sett on a lytle before the beginning and to stay thereon a lytle after the end."

The disgrace of the pillory clung, though the offence punished was not disgraceful. Thus in the year 1697 a citizen of Braintree, William Veasey, was set in the pillory for ploughing on a Thanksgiving day, which had been appointed in gratitude for the escape of King William from assassination. The stiff old Braintree rebel declared that James II was his rightful king. Five years later Veasey was elected a member of the General Court, but was not permitted to serve as he had been in the pillory.

Throughout the Massachusetts jurisdiction the pillory was in use. In 1671 one Mr. Thomas Withers for "surriptisiously endeavoring to prevent the Providence of God by putting in several votes for himself as an officer at a town meeting" was ordered to stand two hours in the pillory at York, Maine. Shortly after (for he was an ingenious rogue) he was similarly punished for "an irregular way of contribution," for putting large sums of money into the contribution box in meeting to induce others to give largely, and then again "surriptisiously" taking his gift back again.

There was no offense in the southern colonies more deplored, more reprobated, more legislated against than what was known as "ingrossing, forestalling, or regrating."

This was what would to-day be termed a brokerage or speculative sale, such as buying a cargo about to arrive, and selling at retail, buying a large quantity of any goods in a

market to re-sell, or any form of huckster-
ing. Its prevalence was held to cause dearth,
famine and despair ; English " regratours"
and forestallers were frequently pilloried.
Even in *Piers Plowman* we read :

" For these aren men on this molde that moste harm
      worcheth,
 To the pore peple that parcel-mele buyggen
 Thei rychen thorow regraterye."

The state archives of Máryland are full of
acts and resolves about forestallers, etc., and
severe punishments were decreed. It was,
in truth, the curse of that colony. All our
merchandise brokers to-day would in those
days have been liable to be thrust in prison
or pillory.

In the year 1648 I learn from the Maryland archives that one John Goneere, for perjury, was " nayled by both eares to the pillory
3 nailes in each eare and the nailes to be slitt
out, and whipped 20 good lashes." The
same year Blanch Howell wilfully, unsolicited
and unasked, committed perjury. The "sd
Blanche shall stand nayled in the Pillory and
loose both her eares." Both those sentences
were " exequuted."

In New York the pillory was used. Under Dutch rule, Mesaack Maartens, accused of stealing cabbages from Jansen, the ship-carpenter living on *'t maagde paatje,* was sentenced to stand in the pillory with cabbages on his head. Truly this was a striking sight. Dishonest bakers were set in the pillory with dough on their heads. At the trial of this Mesaack Maartens, he was tortured to make him confess. Other criminals in New York bore torture; a sailor—wrongfully, as was proven —a woman, for stealing stockings. At the time of the Slave Riots cruel tortures were inflicted. Yet to Massachusetts, under the excitement and superstition caused by that tragedy in New England history, the witchcraft trials, is forever accorded the disgrace that one of her citizens was pressed to death, one Giles Corey. The story of his death is too painful for recital.

Mr. Channing wrote an interesting account of the Newport of the early years of this century. He says of crimes and criminals in that town at that time:

" The public modes of punishment established by law were four, viz.: executions by hanging, whipping of men at the cart-tail, whipping of women in the jail-yard, and the elevation of counterfeiters and the like to a movable pillory, which turned on its base so as to front north, south, east and west in succession, remaining at each point a quarter of an hour. During this execution of the majesty of the law the neck of the culprit was bent to a most uncomfortable curve, presenting a facial mark for those salutations of stale eggs which seemed to have been preserved for the occasion. The place selected for the infliction of this punishment was in front of the State House."

A conviction and sentence in Newport in 1771 was thus reported in the daily newspapers, among others the *Essex Gazette* of April 23:

"William Carlisle was convicted of passing Counterfeit Dollars, and sentenced to stand One Hour in the Pillory on Little-Rest Hill, next Friday, to have both Ears cropped, to be branded on both Cheeks with the Letter R, to pay a fine of One Hundred Dollars and Cost of Prosecution, and to stand committed till Sentence performed."

Severe everywhere were the punishments awarded to counterfeiters. The Continental bills bore this line: "To counterfeit this bill is Death." In 1762 Jeremiah Dexter of Walpole, for passing on two counterfeit dollars, "knowing them to be such," stood in the pillory for an hour; another rogue, for the same offense, had his ears cropped.

Mr. Samuel Breck, speaking of methods of punishment in his boyhood in Boston, in 1771, said:

"A little further up State Street was to be seen the pillory with three or four fellows fastened by the head and hands, and standing for an hour in that helpless posture, exposed to gross and cruel jeers from the multitude, who pelted them constantly with rotten eggs and every repulsive kind of garbage that could be collected."

Instances of punishment in Boston by the pillory of both men and women are many. In the *Boston Post-Boy* of February, 1763, I read:

"BOSTON, JANUARY 31.—At the Superiour Court held at Charlestown last Week, Samuel Bacon of Bedford, and Meriam

Fitch wife of Benjamin Fitch of said Bedford, were convicted of being notorious Cheats, and of having by Fraud, Craft and Deceit, possess'd themselves of Fifteen Hundred Johannes the property of a third Person; were sentenced to be each of them set in the Pillory one Hour, with a Paper on each of their Breasts and the words A CHEAT wrote in Capitals thereon, to suffer three months' imprisonment, and to be bound to their good Behaviour for one Year and to pay Costs."

From the *Boston Chronicle*, November 20, 1769:

"We learn from Worcester that on the eighth instant one Lindsay stood in the Pillory there one hour, after which he received 30 stripes at the public whipping-post, and was then branded in the hand his crime was Forgery."

The use of the pillory in New England extended into this century. On the 15th of January, 1801, one Hawkins, for the crime of forgery, stood for an hour in a pillory in Salem, and had his ears cropped. The pillory was in use in Boston, certainly as late as

1803. In March of that year the brigantine "Hannah" was criminally sunk at sea by its owner Robert Pierpont and its master H. R. Story, to defraud the underwriters. The two criminals were sentenced after trial to stand one hour in the pillory in State Street on two days, be confined in prison for two years and pay the costs of the prosecution. As this case was termed "a transaction exceeding in infamy all that has hitherto appeared in the commerce of our country," this sentence does not seem severe.

The pillory lingered long in England. Lord Thurlow was eloquent in its defence, calling it "the restraint against licentiousness provided by the wisdom of past ages." In 1812 Lord Ellenborough, equally warm in his approval and endorsement, sentenced a blasphemer to the pillory for two hours, once each month, for eighteen months; and in 1814 he ordered Lord Cochrane, the famous sea-fighter of Brasque Roads fame, to be set in the pillory for spreading false news. But Sir Francis Burdett declared he would stand on the pillory by Lord Cochrane's side, and public opinion was more powerful than the Judge. By this time the pillory was rarely used save in cases of perjury. As late as 1830 a man was pilloried for that crime. In 1837 the pillory was ordered to be abandoned, by Act of Parliament; and in 1832 it was abolished in France.

V

PUNISHMENTS OF AUTHORS
AND BOOKS.

The punishments of authors deserve a separate chapter; for since the days of Greece and Rome their woes have been many. The burning of condemned books begun in those ancient states. In the days of Augustus no less than twenty thousand volumes were consumed; among them, all the works of Labienus, who, in despair thereat, refused food, pined and died. His friend Cassius Severus, when he heard sentence pronounced, cried out in a loud voice that they must burn him also if they wished the books to perish, as he knew them all by heart.

The Bible fed the flames by order of Dioclesian. And in England the public hangman warmed his marrow at both literary and religious flames. Bishop Stockesly caused all the New Testament of Tindal's translation to be openly burnt in St. Paul's churchyard. On August 27, 1659, Milton's books were burnt by the hangman; Marlow's translations kept company. These vicarious sufferings were as nothing in the recital of the author's woes, for the sight of an author or a publisher with his ear nailed to a pillory was too common to be widely noted, for anyone who printed without permission could, by the law of the land, be thus treated ; when the author was released, if his bleeding ear was left on the pillory, that did not matter. The rise of the Puritans and their public expression of faith is marked by most painful episodes for those unterrified men. Dr. Leighton, who wrote *Zion's Plea Against Prelacy*, paid dearly for calling the Queen a daughter of Heth, and Episcopacy satanical. He was degraded from the ministry, pilloried, branded, whipped, his ear was cut off, his nostril slit ; he was fined £10,000 and languished eleven years in prison, only to be told on his tardy release, with the irony of fate, that his mutilation and imprisonment had been illegal.

In 1664 Benjamin Keach, a Baptist minister, was arraigned for writing and publishing

a seditious book. His arrest was brought
about by another minister named Disney,
who, as his fellow-countrymen would say,
" sings small" in the matter. Disney wrote
" to his honoured friend Luke Wilkes, esqre,
at Whitehall, with speed, these presents " :
" Honour'd Sir And Loving Brother :

This Primmer owned by Benjamin Keach
as the Author and bought by my man George
Chilton for five pence of Henry Keach of
Stableford Mill neare me, a miller ; who then
sayd that his brother Benjamin Keach is
author of it, and that there are fiveteen hundred of them printed. This Benjamin Keach
is a Tayler, and one that is a teacher in this
new-fangled-way and lives at Winslow a
market town in Buckingnamshire. Pray take
some speedie course to acquaint my Lord
Archbishop his Grace with it, whereby his
authoritye may issue forth that ye impression
may be seized upon before they be much more
dispersed to ye poisoning of people ; they
containing (as I conceive) schismaticall fac-
tions and hereticall matter. Some are scat-
tered in my parish, and perchance in no place
sooner because he hath a sister here and some

others of his gang, two whereof I have bought up. Pray let me have your speedie account of it. I doubt not but it will be taken as acceptable service to God's church and beleeve it a very thankeful obligement to

> Honoured Sir,
>> Your truely Loving Brother,"
>>> THOMAS DISNEY.

As a result of Disney's neighborly and zealous offices, Benjamin Keach was thus sentenced:

" That you shall go to gaol for a fortnight without bail or mainprise; and the next Saturday to stand upon the pillory at Ailsbury for the space of two hours, from eleven o'clock to one, with a paper on your head with this inscription: *For writing, printing and publishing a schismatical book, entitled 'The Child's Instructor; or, a New and Easy Primmer.'* And the next Thursday so stand, and in the same manner and for the same time, in the market of Winslow; and there your book shall be openly burnt before your face by the common hangman, in disgrace to you and your doctrine. And you shall forfeit to the King's Majesty the sum of £20, and shall remain in gaol till you find securities for your good behaviour and appearance at the next assizes, there to renounce your doctrine and to make such public submission as may be enjoined you."

Keach stood twice with head and hands set in the pillory, and his book was burnt, and his fine was paid; but never was he subdued, and never did he make recantation."

Pope wrote a well-known, oft-quoted, yet false line :

" Earless on high stood unabashed De Foe."

The great Daniel De Foe did stand on high on a pillory, but he was not earless. He was by birth and belief a Dissenter, and he wrote a severe satire against the Church party, entitled *The Shortest Way with the Dissenters*, which so ironically, and with such apparent soberness, reduced the argument of the intolerant to an absurdity, that for a short time it deceived zealous church-folk, who welcomed and praised it, but who turned on him with redoubled hatred when they finally perceived the satire. It was termed a scandalous and seditious pamphlet, and fifty pounds reward was offered for him. He was arrested, tried, pilloried in three places, and imprisoned for a year; but the Queen paid his fine for his release from prison, and his pillory was hung with garlands of flowers, and his health was drunk, and scraps of his vigorous doggerel from his *Hymn to the Pillory* passed from lip to lip.

" Men that are men in thee can feel no pain
   And all thy insignificants disdain
      Contempt that false new word for shame
      Is, without crime, an empty name.

   The first intent of laws
Was to correct the effect and check the cause
   And all the ends of punishment
Were only future mischiefs to prevent.

   But justice is inverted when
      Those engines of the law
   Instead of pinching vicious men
      Keep honest ones in awe.''

Williams, the bookseller, set in the pillory in the year 1765 for republishing the *North Briton* was also treated with marks of consideration and kindness. He held a sprig of laurel in his hand as he stood, and a purse of two hundred guineas for his benefit was collected in the crowd.

As times changed, so did opinions. The Bishop of Rochester denounced Martin Luther and all his works, and Luther's books were burned in the public squares. Puritan publications by the hundreds fed the flames; Quaker and Baptist books took their turns. Then the Parliamentary soldiers burned the Book of Common Prayer. In France, in the year 1790, the monasteries were ransacked and their books burned. In Paris eight hundred thousand were burned; in all France over four million: of these twenty-six thousand were in manuscript.

Crossing the Atlantic to a land void of printing presses could not silence Puritan authors. They still had pen and ink, and manuscripts could be sent back across the ocean to a land full of presses and type.

A rather amusing episode of early Massachusetts history anent authors happened in 1634, as may be found in Volume I, page 137, of the *Colonial Records*.

" Whereas Mr. Israel Stoughton hath written a certain book, which hath occasioned much trouble and offence to the Court; the said Mr. Stoughton did desire of the court, that the said book might be burnt, as being weak and offensive."

Such extraordinary and unparalleled modesty on the part of an author did not save Mr. Stoughton's bacon, for he was disabled from holding any office in the commonwealth for the space of three years. Winthrop said he used "weak arguments," all of which did not prevent his being a brave soldier in the Pequot Wars, and serving as a colonel in the Parliamentary army in England.

A fuller account of the trials of a Puritan author in a new land is told through notes taken from the court records. First may be given a declaration of the Court:

"The Generall Court, now sitting at Boston, in New England, this sixteenth of October, 1650. There was brought to or hands a booke writen, as was therein subscribed, to William Pinchon, Gent, in New England, entituled The Meritorious Price of or Redemption, Justifycation, &c. clearinge it from some common Errors &c. which booke, brought ouer hither by a shippe a few dayes since and contayninge many errors & heresies generally condemned by all orthodox writers

that we haue met with and haue judged it
meete and necessary, for vindicatio of the truth,
so far as in vs lyes, as also to keepe & pserue
the people here committed to or care & trust
in the true knowledge & faythe of or Lord
Jesus Christ, & of or owne redemption by
him, and likewise for the clearinge of orselves
to or Christian brethren & others in England,
(where this booke was printed & is dispersed),
hereby to ptest or innocency, as being neither
partyes nor priuy to the writinge, composinge,
printinge, nor diuulging thereof; but that, on
the contrary, we detest & abhorre many of
the opinions & assertions therein as false,
eronyous, & hereticall; yea, & whatsoeuer is
contayned in the sd booke which are contrary to the Scriptures ofthe Old & New
Testament, & the generall received doctrine
ofthe orthodox churches extant since the
time ofthe last & best reformation & for
proffe and euidence of or sincere & playne
meaninge therein, we doe hereby condemne
the sd booke to be burned in the market
place, at Boston, by the common execu-
tionor, & doe purpose with all convenient
speede to convent the sd William Pinehon

before authority, to find out whether the sd
William Pinchon will owne the sd booke as
his or not; which if he doth, we purpose
(Gd willinge) to pceede with him accordinge
to his demerits, vnles he retract the same,
and giue full satisfaction both here & by
some second writinge to be printed and dispersed in England; all of which we thought
needfull, for the reasons aboue aleaged, to
make knowne by this short ptestation & declaration. Also we further purpose, with
what convenient speede we may, to appoynt
some fitt psn to make a pticuler answer to
all materiall & controuersyall passages in the
sd booke, & to publish the same in print, that
so the errors & falsityes therein may be fully
discoued, the truth cleared, & the minds of
those that loue & seeke after truth confirmed
therein p curia."

"It is agreed vppon by the whole Court,
that Mr. Norton, one of the reuend elders of
Ipswich, should be intreated to answer Mr.
Pinchon's booke with all convenient speed."

The sentence of this book to be burned by
the common hangman was changed to be
burned by some person appointed to the duty

who would consent to perform it. It was not always easy to get a hangman.

In 1684 a man in Maryland "of tender years" was convicted of horse-stealing and sentenced to death. A "private and secret" pardon was issued by the Assembly, but he was given no knowledge of it until he was conveyed to the place of execution and the rope placed round his neck, when he was respited on condition that he would perform the part for life of common hangman, which he did.

The hangman was usually some respited prisoner under sentence of death. In some shires in England, he had to be hung at last himself, else the power of possessing a hangman lapsed from the town. One hangman, mortally sick, was bolstered up by his friends with a shoemaker's bench and kit in front or him, pretending to work, and when the sheriffs came to seize him and carry him to the gallows, he did not seem very sick and they left the house without him. He died that night peaceably in bed. All these doings seem too barbarous for civilized England.

Thomas Maule was a Salem Quaker and

an author. His book was ordered to be
burned in 1695 in Boston market place.
The diary of the Reverend Dr. Bentley says
of him :

" Tho's Maule, shopkeeper of Salem, is
brought before the Council to answer for his
printing and publishing a pamphlet of 260
pages entitled " Truth held Forth and Main-
tained," owns the book but will not own all,
till he sees his copy which is at New York
with Bradford who printed it. Saith he writt
to ye Gov'r of N. York before he could get
it printed. Book is ordered to be burnt —
being stuff'd wth notorious lyes and scandals,
and he recognizes to it next Court of Assize
and gen'l gaol delivery to be held for the
County of Essex. He acknowledges that
what was written concerning the circum-
stance of Major Gen. Atherton's death was
a mistake, was chiefly insisted on against
him, which I believe was a surprize to him,
he expecting to be examined in some point of
religion, as should seem by his bringing his
Bible under his arm."

In 1654 the writings of John Reeves and
Ludowick Muggleton, self-styled prophets,

were burned in Boston market-place by that abhorred public functionary the hangman. Other Quaker books were similarly burned, and John Rogers of New London, who hated the Quakers, but whom the Boston magistrates persisted in regarding and classifying as a Quaker, had to see his books perish in the flames in company with Quaker publications. In 1754 a pamphlet called *The Monster of Monsters*, a sharp criticism on the Massachusetts Court which caused much stir in provincial political circles, was burned by the hangman in King Street, Boston. We learn from the *Connecticut Gazette* that about the same time another offending publication was sentenced to be "publickly whipt according to Moses Law, with forty stripes save one, and then burnt." The true book-lover winces at the thought of the blood-stained hands of the hangman on any book, even though a "Monster."

VI

THE WHIPPING–POST

John Taylour, the " Water-Poet," wrote in 1630:

" In London, and within a mile, I ween
  There are jails or prisons full fifteen
  And sixty whipping-posts and stocks and cages."

Church and city records throughout England show how constantly these whipping-posts were made to perform their share of legal and restrictive duties. In the reign of Henry VIII a famous Whipping Act had been passed by which all vagrants were to be whipped severely at the cart-tail " till the body became bloody by reason of such whipping." This enactment remained in force nearly through the reign of Elizabeth, when the whipping-post became the usual substitute for the cart, but the force of the blows was not lightened.

The poet Cowper has left in one of his

Whipping at
the Cart's Tayle.

letters an amusing account of a sanguinary whipping which he witnessed. The thief had stolen some ironwork at a fire at Olney in 1783, and had been tried, and sentenced to be whipped at the cart-tail.

" The fellow seemed to show great fortitude, but it was all an imposition. The beadle who whipped him had his left hand filled with red ochre, through which, after every stroke, he drew the lash of the whip, leaving the appearance of a wound upon the skin, but in reality not hurting him at all. This being perceived by the constable who followed the beadle to see that he did his duty, he (the constable) applied the cane without any such management or precaution to the shoulders of the beadle. The scene now became interesting and exciting. The beadle could by no means be induced to strike the thief hard, which provoked the constable to strike harder; and so the double flogging continued until a lass of Silver End, pitying the pityful beadle thus suffering under the hands of the pityless constable, joined the procession, and placing herself immediately behind the constable seized him by his capillary pigtail, and pulling him backwards by the same, slapped his face with Amazonian fury. This concentration of events has taken more of my paper than I intended, but I could not forbear to inform you how the beadle thrashed the thief, the constable the beadle, and the lady the constable, and how the thief was the only person who suffered nothing."

As a good, sound British institution, and to have familiar home-like surroundings in the new strange land, the whipping-post was promptly set up, and the whip set at work in all the American colonies. In the orders sent over from England for the restraint of the first settlement at Salem, whipping was enjoined, " as correcçon is ordaned for the fooles back "—and fools' backs soon were found for the " correcçon "; tawny skins and white shared alike in punishment, as both Indians and white men were partakers in crime. Scourgings were sometimes given on Sabbath days and often on lecture days, to the vast content and edification of Salem folk.

The whipping-post was speedily in full force in Boston. At the session of the court held November 30, 1630, one man was sentenced to be whipped for stealing a loaf of bread; another for shooting fowl on the Sabbath, another for swearing, another for leaving a boat " without a pylott." Then we read of John Pease that for " stryking his mother and deryding her he shalbe whipt."

In 1631, in June, this order was given by the General Court in Boston :

" That Philip Ratcliffe shall be whipped, have his eares cutt off, fined 40 pounds, and banished out of the limits of this jurisdiction, for uttering malicious and scandalous speeches against the Government."

Governor Winthrop added to his account of this affair that Ratcliffe was " convict of most foul slanderous invectives against our government." This episode and the execution of this sentence caused much reprehension and unfavorable comment in England, where, it would seem, whipping and ear-lopping were rife enough to be little noted. But the mote in our brother's eye seemed very large when seen across the water. Anent it, in a letter written from London to the Governor's son, I read : " I have heard divers complaints against the severity of your government, about cutting off the lunatick man's ears and other grievances."

In 1630 Henry Lynne of Boston was sentenced to be whipped. He wrote to England "against the government and execution of justice here," and was again whipped and banished. Lying, swearing, taking false toll, perjury, selling rum to the Indians, all were punished by whipping.

Pious regard for the Sabbath was fiercely upheld by the support of the whipping-post. In 1643 Roger Scott, for "repeated sleeping on the Lord's Day" and for striking the person who waked him from his godless slumber was sentenced to be severely whipped.

Women were not spared in public chastisement. "The gift of prophecy" was at once subdued in Boston by lashes, as was unwomanly carriage. On February 30, 1638, this sentence was rendered:

"Anne ux. Richard Walker being cast out of the church of Boston for intemperate drinking from one inn to another, and for light and wanton behavior, was the next day called before the governour and the treasurer, and convict by two witnesses, and was stripped

74

naked one shoulder, and tied to the whipping-post, but her punishment was respited."

Every year, every month, and in time every week, fresh whippings followed. No culprits were, however, to be beaten more than forty stripes as one sentence; and the *Body of Liberties* decreed that no " true gentleman or any man equall to a gentleman shall be punished with whipping unless his crime be very shameful and his course of life vitious and profligate." In pursuance of this notion of the exemption of the aristocracy from bodily punishment, a Boston witness testified in one flagrant case, as a condonement of the offense, that the culprit " had been a soldier and was a gentleman and they must have their liberties," and he urged letting the case default, and to " make no uprore " in the matter. The lines of social position were just as well defined in New England as in old England, else why was one Mr. Plaistowe, for fraudulently obtaining corn from the Indians, condemned as punishment to be called Josias instead of Mr. as heretofore? His servant, who assisted in the fraud, was whipped. A Maine man named Thomas

Taylour for his undue familiarity shown in his "theeing and thouing" Captain Raynes was set in the stocks.

Slander and name-calling were punished by whipping. On April 1, 1634, John Lee "for calling Mr. Ludlowe false-heart knave, hard-heart knave, heavy ffriend shalbe whipt and fyned XIs." Six months later he was again in hot water:

"John Lee shalbe whipt and fyned for speaking reproachfully of the Governor, saying hee was but a lawyer's clerk, and what understanding hadd hee more than himselfe, also takeing the Court for makeing lawes to picke men's purses, also for abusing a mayd of the Governor, pretending love in the way of marriage when himselfe professed hee intended none."

In the latter clause of this count against John Lee doubtless lay the sting of his offenses. For Governor Winthrop was very solicitous of the ethics of love-making, and to deceive the affections of one of his fen-county English serving-lasses was to him without doubt a grave misdemeanor.

Those harmless and irresponsible creatures,

young lovers, were menaced with the whip. Read this extract from the Plymouth Laws, dated 1638:

" Whereas divers persons unfit for marriage both in regard of their yeong yeares, as also in regarde of their weake estate, some practiseing the inveagling of men's daughters and maids under gardians contrary to their parents and gardians likeing, and of maide servants, without the leave and likeing of their masters: It is therefore enacted by the Court that if any shall make a motion of marriage to any man's daughter or mayde servant, not having first obtayned leave and consent of the parents or master soe to doe, shall be punished either by fine or corporall punishment, or both, at the discretions of the bench, and according to the nature of the offense."

The New Haven Colony, equally severe on unlicensed lovemaking, specified the " inveagling," whether done by " speech, writing, message, company-keeping, unnecessary familiarity, disorderly night meetings, sinfull dalliance, gifts or, (as a final blow to inventive lovers) in any other way."

The New Haven magistrates had early given their word in favor of a whipping-post, in these terms:

" Stripes and whippings is a correction fit and proper in some cases where the offense is accompanied with childish or brutish folly, or rudeness, or with stubborn insolency or bestly cruelty, or with idle vagrancy, or for faults of like nature."

In the " Pticuler" Court of Connecticut this entry appears. The " wounding" was of the spirit not of the body:

" May 12, 1668. Nicholas Wilton for wounding the wife of John Brooks, and Mary Wilton the wife of Nicholas Wilton, for contemptuous and reproachful terms by her put on one of the Assistants are adjudged she to be whipt 6 stripes upon the naked body next training day at Windsor and the said Nicholas is hereby disfranchised of his freedom in this Corporation, and to pay for the Horse and Man that came with him to the Court to-day, and for what damage he hath done to the said Brooks His wife, and sit in the stocks the same day his wife is to receive her punishment."

The Whipping Post

In New York a whipping-post was set up on the strand, in front of the Stadt Huys, under Dutch rule, and sentences were many. A few examples of the punishment under the Dutch may be given. A sailmaker, rioting in drink around New Amsterdam cut one Van Brugh on the jaw. He was sentenced to be fastened to a stake, severely scourged and a gash made in his left cheek, and to be banished. To the honor of Vrouw Van Brugh let me add that she requested the court that these penalties should not be carried out, or at any rate done in a closed room. One Van ter Goes for treasonable words of great flagrancy was brought with a rope round his neck to a half-gallows, whipped, branded and banished. Roger Cornelisen for theft was scourged in public, while Herman Barenson, similarly accused was so loud in his cries for mercy that he was punished with a rod in a room. From a New York newspaper, dated 1712, I learn that one woman at the whipping-post "created much amusement by her resistance" —which statement throws a keen light on the cold-blooded and brutal indifference of the times to human suffering.

May 14, 1750, *New York Gazette.*

"Tuesday last one David Smith was convicted in the Mayor's Court of Taking or stealing Goods off a Shop Window in this City, and was sentenced to be whipped at the Carts Tail round this Town and afterwards whipped at the Pillory which sentence was accordingly executed on him."

In the same paper, date October 2, 1752, an account is given of the pillorying of a boy for picking pockets and the whipping of an Irishman for stealing deerskins. Another man was "whipt round the city" for stealing a barrel of flour: In January, 1761, four men for "petty larceny" were whipped at the cart-tail round New York.

In 1638 a whipping post was set up in Portsmouth, New Hampshire, as a companion to the cage. For "speaking opprobriously," and even for "suspitious speeches," New Haven citizens were whipped at the "carts podex."

Rhode Island even under the tolerant and gentle Roger Williams had no idle whip. "Larcenie," drunkenness, perjury, were punished at the whipping-post. In Newport malefac-

tors were whipped at the cart-tail until this
century. Mr. Channing tells of seeing them
fastened to the cart and being thus slowly led
through the streets to a public spot where
they were whipped on the naked back.
Women were at that time whipped in the
jail-yard with only spectators of their own
sex.

In Plymouth women were whipped at the
cart-tail, and the towns resounded with the
blows dealt out to Quakers. In 1636, on a
day in June, one Helin Billinton, was whipped
in Plymouth for slander.

There was a whipping-post on Queen
Street in Boston, another on the Common,
another on State Street, and they were constantly in use in Boston in Revolutionary
times. Samuel Breck wrote of the year 1771 :

" The large whipping-post painted red
stood conspicuously and prominently in the
most public street in the town. It was
placed in State Street directly under the win-
dows of a great writing school which I fre-
quented, and from there the scholars were
indulged in the spectacle of all kinds of punishment suited to harden their hearts and

brutalize their feelings. Here women were taken in a huge cage in which they were dragged on wheels from prison, and tied to the post with bare backs on which thirty or forty lashes were bestowed among the screams of the culprit and the uproar of the mob."

The diary of a Boston school-girl of twelve, little Anna Green Winslow, written the same year as Mr. Breck's account, gives a detailed account of the career of one Bet Smith, through workhouse and gaol to whipping-post, and thence to be "set on the gallows where she behaved with great impudence."

Criminals were sentenced in lots. On September 9, 1787, in one Boston court one burglar was sentenced to be hanged, five thieves to be whipped, two greater thieves to be set on the gallows, and one counterfeiter set on the pillory.

Cowper's account of the tender-hearted beadle is supplemented by a similiar peformance in Boston as shown in a Boston paper of August 11, 1789. Eleven culprits were to receive in one day the "discipline of the post." Another criminal was obtained by the Sheriff to inflict the punishment, but he persisted in being "tender of strokes," though ordered by the Sheriff to lay on. At last the Sheriff seized the whip and lashed the whipper, then turned to the row of ninepins and delivered the lashes. "The citizens who were assembled complimented the Sheriff with three cheers for the manly determined manner in which he executed his duty."

So common were whippings in the southern colonies at the date of settlement of the country, that in Virginia even "launderers and launderesses" who "dare to wash any uncleane Linen, drive bucks, or throw out the water or suds of fowle clothes in the open streetes," or who took pay for washing for a soldier or laborer, or who gave old torn linen for good linen, were severely whipped. Many other offenses were punished by whipping in Virginia, such as slitting the ears of hogs, or cutting off the ends of hogs' ears — thereby removing ear-marks and destroying claim to perambulatory property — stealing tobacco, running away from home, drunkenness, destruction of land-marks ; and in 1664 Major Robins brought suit against one Mary Powell for " scandalous speaches " against Rev. Mr.

Teackle, for which she was ordered to receive twenty lashes on her bare shoulders and to be banished the country. Of course, for the correction of slaves the whip was in constant use till our Civil War banished slavery and the whipping-post from every state save Maryland and Delaware. This latter-named commonwealth has been much censured for countenancing the continuance of whipping as a punishment. It is, however, stiffly contended by Delaware magistrates that as a restraint over wife-beaters and other cruel and vicious criminals, the whipping post is a distinct success and of marked benefit in its influence in the community. It should also be remembered that these are not the only civilized states to approve of whipping for certain crimes. About thirty years ago, when garroting became so frequent and so greatly feared in England, the whipping-post was re-established in England, and whipping once more became an authorized punishment.

There was one hard-hearted and unjust use of the whip which was prevalent in London and other English cities in olden times which I wish to recount with abjuration. At the time of public executions parents were wont to whip their children soundly to impress upon them a lesson of horror of the gallows. As trivial offenses, such as stealing anything in value over a shilling, were punishable by death, and capital crimes were over three hundred in number, executions were of deplorable frequency; hence the condition of children at that time was indeed pitiable. Whipped by most illogical parents, whipped by cruel teachers — even Roger Ascham used to "pinch, nip and bob" Queen Elizabeth when she was his pupil — whipped by masters, whipped by mistresses, it would seem that the moral force of the whipping-post for adults must have been very slight, after so many castigory experiences in youth.

VII

THE SCARLET LETTER

The rare genius of Hawthorne has immortalized in his *Scarlet Letter* one mode of stigmatizing punishment common in New England. So faithful is the presentment of colonial life shown in that book, so unerring the power and touch which drew the picture, it cannot be disputed that the atmosphere of the *Scarlet Letter* forms in the majority of hearts, nay, in the hearts and minds of all of our reading community, the daily life, the true life of the earliest colonists. To us the characters have lived — Hester Prynne is as real as Margaret Winthrop, Arthur Dimmesdale as John Cotton.

The glorified letter that stands out of the pages of that book had its faithful and painful prototype in real life in all the colonies; humbler in its fashioning, worn less nobly, endured more despairingly, it shone a scarlet brand on the breast of those real Hesters.

The Scarlet Letter.

It was characteristic of the times — every little Puritan community sought to know by every fireside, to hate in every heart, any offence, great or small, which could hinder the growth and prosperity of the new abiding-place, which was to all a true home, and which they loved with a fervor that would be incomprehensible did we not know their spiritual exaltation in their new-found freedom to worship God.   Since they were human, they sinned.   But the sinners were never spared, either in publicity or punishment.   Keen justice made the magistrates rigid and exact in the exposition and publication of crime, hence the labelling of an offender.

From the Colony Records of " New Plymouth," dated June, 1671, we find that Pilgrim Hester Prynnes were thus enjoined by those stern moralists the magistrates :

" To wear two Capitall Letters, A. D. cut in cloth and sewed on their uppermost garment on the Arm and Back ; and if any time they shall be founde without the letters so worne while in this government, they shall be forthwith taken and publickly whipt."

Many examples could be gathered from

early court records of the wearing of significant letters by criminals.   In 1656 a woman
was sentenced to be " whipt at Taunton and
Plymouth on market day."   She was also to
be fined and forever in the future " to have a
Roman B cutt out of ridd cloth & sewed to
her vper garment on her right arm in sight."
This was for blasphemous words.   In 1638
John Davis of Boston was ordered to wear a
red V " on his vpermost garment"—which
signified, I fancy, viciousness.   In 1636 William Bacon was sentenced to stand an hour
in the pillory wearing " in publique vew" a
great D—for his habitual drunkenness.
Other drunkards suffered similar punishment.
On September 3, 1633, in Boston :

" Robert Coles was fyned ten shillings and
enjoyned to stand with a white sheet of paper
on his back whereon Drunkard shalbe written in great lres & to stand therewith soe
longe as the Court finde meete, for abuseing
himself shamefully with drinke."

The following year Robert Coles, still mis-
behaving, was again sentenced, and more
severely, for his drunkard's badge was made
permanent.

" 1634. Robert Coles, for drunkenes by him comitted at Rocksbury, shalbe disfranchized, weare about his necke, & soe to hange vpon his outwd garment a D. made of redd cloth & sett vpon white ; to continyu this for a yeare, and not to have itt off any time hee comes among company, Vnder the penalty of xls for the first offence & v£ for the second & afterwards to be punished by the Court as they think meete, alsoe hee is to weare the D. outwards."

We might be justified in drawing an inference from the latter clause that some mortified wearers of a scarlet letter had craftily turned it away from public gaze, hoping thus to escape public odium and ostracism.

Paupers were plainly labelled, as was the custom everywhere in England. In New York, the letters N. Y. showed to what town they submitted. In Virginia this law was in force :

" That every person who shall receive relief from the parish, and be sent to the said house, shall, upon the shoulder of the right sleeve of his or her uppermost garment, in an open and visible manner, wear a badge with the name of the parish to which he or she belongs, cut in red, blue or green cloth, as the vestry or church wardens shall direct ; and if any poor person shall neglect or refuse to wear such badge, such offence may be punished either by ordering his or her allowance to be abridged, suspended or withdrawn, or the offender to be whipped not exceeding five lashes for one offence; and if any person not entitled to relief, as aforesaid, shall presume to wear such badge, he or she shall be whipped for every such offence."

The conditions of wearing "in an open and visible manner" may have been a legal concession necessitated by the action of the English goody who, when ordered to wear a pauper's badge, demurely pinned it on an under-petticoat.

A more limited and temporary mortification of a transgressor consisted in the marking by significant letters or labels inscribed in large letters with the name or nature of the crime. These were worn only while the offender was exposed to public view or ridicule in cage, or upon pillory, stocks, gallows or penance stool, or on the meeting house steps, or in the market-place.

An early and truly characteristic law for those of Puritan faith reads thus :

" If any interrupt or oppose a preacher in season of worship, they shall be reproved by the Magistrate, and on a repetition, shall pay £5 or stand two hours on a block four feet high, with this inscription in Capitalls, A WANTON GOSPELLER."

This law was enacted in Boston. A similar one was in force in the Connecticut colony. In 1650 a man was tried in the General Court in Hartford for " contemptuous carriages " against the church and ministers, and was thus sentenced :

" To stand two houres openly upon a blocke or stoole foure feet high uppon a Lecture Daye with a paper fixed on his breast written in Capitall Letters, AN OPEN AND OBSTINATE CONTEMNER OF GOD'S HOLY ORDINANCES, that others may feare and be ashamed of breakinge out in like wickednesse."

The latter clause would seem to modern notions an unintentional yet positive appeal to the furtherance of time-serving and hypocrisy.

Drunkards frequently were thus temporarily labelled.

I quote an entry of Governor Winthrop's in the year 1640:

" One Baker, master's mate of the ship, being in drink, used some reproachful words of the queen. The governour and council were much in doubt what to do with him, but having considered that he was distempered, and sorry for it, and being a stranger, and a chief officer in the ship, and many ships were there in harbour, they thought it not fit to inflict corporal punishment upon him, but after he had been two or three days in prison, he was set an hour at the whipping post with a paper on his head and dismissed."

Many Boston men were similarly punished. For defacing a public record one was sentenced in May, 1652, " to stand in the pillory two Howers in Boston market with a paper ouer his head marked in Capitall Letters A DEFACER OF RECORDS." Ann Boulder at about the same time was ordered " to stand in yrons half an hour with a Paper on her Breast marked PVBLICK DESTROYER OF PEACE."

In 1639 three Boston women received this form of public punishment; of them Margaret Henderson was "censured to stand in the market place with a paper for her ill behavior, & her husband was fyned £5 for her yvill behavior & to bring her to the market place for her to stand there."

Joan Andrews of York, Maine, sold two heavy stones in a firkin of butter. She, too, had to stand disgraced bearing the description of her wicked cheatery "written in Capitall Letters and pinned upon her forehead." Widow Bradley of New London, Connecticut, for her sorry behaviour in 1673 had to wear a paper pinned to her cap to proclaim her shame.

Really picturesque was Jan of Leyden, of the New Netherland settlement, who for insolence to the Bushwyck magistrates was sentenced to be fastened to a stake near the gallows, with a bridle in his mouth, a bundle of rods under his arm, and a paper on his breast bearing the words, "Lampoon-riter, False-accuser, Defamer of Magistrates." William Gerritsen of New Amsterdam sang a defamatory song against the Lutheran minister and his daughter. He pleaded guilty, and was bound to the Maypole in the Fort with rods tied round his neck, and wearing a paper labelled with his offense, and there to stand till the end of the sermon.

This custom of labelling a criminal with words or initials expositive of his crime or his political or religious offense, is neither American nor Puritan in invention and operation, but is so ancient that the knowledge of its beginning is lost. It was certainly in full force in the twelfth century in England. In 1364 one John de Hakford, for stating to a friend that there were ten thousand rebels ready to rise in London, was placed in the pillory four times a year "without hood or girdle, barefoot and unshod, with a whetstone hung by a chain from his neck, and lying on his breast, it being marked with the words *A False Liar*, and there shall be a pair of trumpets trumpeting before him on his way." Many other cases are known of hanging an inscribed whetstone round the neck of the condemned one. For three centuries men were thus labelled, and with sound of trumpets borne to the pillory or scaffold. As few of the spectators of that day could read the printed letters, the whetstone and trumpets were quite as significant as the labels. In the first year of the reign of Henry VIII, Fabian says that three men, rebels, and of good birth, died of shame for being thus punished. They rode about the city of London with their faces to their horses' tails, and bore marked papers on their heads, and were set on the pillory at Cornhill and again at Newgate. In Canterbury, in 1524, a man was pilloried, and wore a paper inscribed : " This is a false perjured and for-sworn man." In the corporation accounts of the town of Newcastle-on-Tyne are many items of the expenses for punishing criminals. One of the date 1594 reads : " Paide for 4 papers for 4 folkes which was sett on the pillorie, 16d."

Writing was not an every-day accomplishment in those times, else fourpence for writing a " paper " would seem rather a high-priced service.

VIII

BRANKS AND GAGS

The brank or scold's bridle was unknown
in America in its English shape: though
from colonial records we learn that scolding
women were far too plentiful, and were
gagged for that annoying and irritating habit.
The brank, sometimes called the gossip's
bridle, or dame's bridle, or scold's helm, was
truly a "brydle for a curste queane." It was
a shocking instrument, a sort of iron cage,
often of great weight; when worn, covering
the entire head; with a spiked plate or flat
tongue of iron to be placed in the mouth
over the tongue. Hence if the offender
spoke she was cruelly hurt.

Ralph Gardner, in his book entitled *Eng-
land's Grievance Discovered in Relation to the
Coal Trade*, *etc.*, printed in 1665, says of
Newcastle-on-Tyne:

"There he saw one Anne Bridlestone

drove through the streets by an officer of the
same corporation, holding a rope in his hand,
the other end fastened to an engine called the
branks, which is like a crown, it being of iron,
which was musled over the head and face,
with a great gag or tongue of iron forced into
her mouth, which forced the blood out; and
that is the punishment which the magistrates do inflict upon chiding and scolding
women; and he hath often seen the like
done to others."

Over fifty branks of various shapes are now
in existence in English museums, churches,
town halls, etc., and prove by their number
and wide extent of location, the prevalence
of their employment as a means of punishment. Being made of durable iron and kept
within doors, and often thrust, as their use
grew infrequent, into out-of-the-way hiding-
places, they have not vanished from existence
as have the wooden stocks and pillories, which
stood exposed to wear, weather and attack.

One of these old-time branks is in the
vestry of the church at Walton-on-Thames.
It is dated 1632, and has this couplet graven
on it:

"Chester presents Walton with a bridle
  To cure women's tongues that talk too idle."

By tradition this brank was angrily and insultingly given by a gentleman named Chester, who had through the lie of a gossiping woman of Walton lost an expected fortune. One is in Congleton Town Hall which was used as recently at 1824, upon a confirmed scold who had especially abused some constables and church-wardens; and as late as 1858 a brank was produced *in terrorem* to silence an English scold, and it is said with marked and salutary effect. Several branks are still in existence in Staffordshire. The old historian of the county, Dr. Plot, pleads quaintly the cause of the brank:

" We come to the arts that respect mankind, amongst which as elsewhere, the civility of precedence must be allowed to the women, and that as well in punishments as in favours. For the former, whereof they have such a peculiar artifice at Newcastle and Walsall for correcting of scolds, which it does too, so effectually and so very safely that I look upon it as much to be preferred to the ducking-stool, which not only endangers the health of the party, but also gives her tongue liberty to wag, twixt every dip, to neither of which is this at all liable, it being such a bridle for the tongue as not only quite deprives them of speech, but brings shame for the transgression, and humility thereupon, before its taken off. . . . . Which being put upon the offender by the order of the magistrate, and fastened with a padlock behind, she is led through the town by an officer, to her shame, nor is it taken off till after the party begins to show all external signs imaginable of humiliation and amendment."

Mr. Llewellyn Jewitt, editor of the *Reliquary*, gives an explicit account of the way a brank was worn :

" The Chesterfield brank is a good example, and has the additional interest of bearing a date. It is nine inches in height, and six and three-quarters across the hoop. It consists of a hoop of iron, hinged on either side, and fastening behind, and a band, also of iron, passing over the head from back to front and opening dividing in front to admit the nose of the woman whose misfortune it was to wear it. The mode of putting it on would be thus: The brank would be opened by throwing back the sides of the hoop, and the hinder part of the top band by means of the hinges. The constable would then stand in front of his victim and force the knife or plate into her mouth, the divided band passing on either side of her nose, which would protrude through the opening. The hoop would then be closed behind, the band brought down from the top to the back of the head, and fastened down upon it, and thus the cage would at once be firmly and immovably fixed so long as her tormentors might think fit. On the left side is a chain, one end of which is attached to the hoop, and on the other end is a ring by which the victim was led, or by which she was at pleasure attached to a post or wall. On the front of the brank is the date 1688."

This brank is depicted in the *Reliquary* for October, 1860. Mr. William Andrews, in his interesting book, entitled *Old-Time Punishments* gives drawings of no less than sixteen branks now preserved in England.

Some of them are massive, and horrible instruments of torture.

It will be noted that the brank is universally spoken of as a punishment for women; but men also were sentenced to wear it — paupers, blasphemers, railers.

I am glad John Winthrop and John Carver did not bring cumbrous and cruel iron branks to America. There are plenty of other ways to shut a woman's mouth and to still her tongue, as all sensible men know; on every hand, if gossips were found, a simple machine could be shaped, one far simpler than a scold's bridle. A cleft stick pinched on the tongue was as temporarily efficacious as the iron machine, and could be speedily put in use. On June 4, 1651, the little town of Southampton, Long Island, saw a well-known resident, for her " exorbitant words of imprication," stand for an hour in public with her tongue in a cleft stick. A neighbor at Easthampton, Long Island, the same year received a like sentence :

"It is ordered that Goody Edwards shall pay £3 or have her tongue in a cleft stick for contempt of court warrant in saienge she would not come, but if they had been governor or magistrate then she would come, and desireing the warrant to burn it."

About the same time Goodwife Hunter was gagged in Springfield for a similar offense.

In Salem, under the sway of the rigid and narrow Puritan Endicott, the system of petty surveillance and demeaning punishment seemed to reach its height; and one citizen in mild sarcasm thereof said he did suppose if he did lie abed in the morning he would be hauled up by the magistrates,— and was promptly fined for even saying such a thing in jest. Therefore of course " one Oliver, his wife " was adjudged to be whipped for reproaching the magistrates and for prophesying. Winthrop, in his *History of New England*, says of her scourging and her further punishment :

" She stood without tying, and bare her punishment with a masculine spirit, glorying in her suffering. But after (when she came to consider the reproach which would stick by her, etc.), she was much dejected about it. She had a cleft stick put on her tongue half an hour for reproaching the elders."

In Salem in 1639 four men got drunk—
young men, some of them servants. Two
named George Dill and John Cook were thus
punished :

" They be fined 40s for drunckenes, and
to stand att the meeting-house doar next Lecture day with a Clefte Stick vpon his Tong
and a paper vpon his hatt subscribed for gross
premeditated lyinge."

The others, Thomas Tucke and Mica
Ivor, were not so drunk nor such wanton
liars and their punishment was somewhat
mitigated. The sentence runs thus:

" They are also found guilty of Lyeing &
Drunckenes though not to that degree as the
twoe former yett are fined 40s & their own
promis taken for itt. Alsoe two stand on
the Lecture day with the twoe former but
noe clefte sticke on their Tong only a paper
on his head subscribed for lying."

So it will be seen that men suffered this
painful and mortifying punishment as well as
women. And I may say, in passing, that
slander and mischief-making seemed to be
even more rife among men than among
women in colonial times. This entry may be

found in the *Records of the Massachusetts Bay Colony*:

"6 September, Boston, 1636. Robert Shorthouse for swearinge by the bloud of God was sentenced to have his tongue put into a cleft stick, and soe stand for halfe an houre & Elizabeth wife of Thomas Applegate was censured to stand with her tongue in a cleft stick for half an houre for swearinge, railinge and revilinge."

Robert Bartlett in the same court in 1638 was "psented" for cursing, and swearing, and had his tongue thrust in a cleft stick. Samuel Hawkes for cursing, lying and stealing received the same sentence. In 1671 Sarah Morgan struck her husband. He evidently ran whining to the constables, and Wife Sarah received a just punishment. She was ordered to "stand with a gagg in her mouth" at Kittery, Maine, at a public town-meeting, and "the cause of her offense written and put on her forehead." Thus gagged and placarded she must have proved a striking figure; jeered at, doubtless, as an odious example of wifely insubordination, by all the good citizens who came to shape the "Town's Mind" at the Town's Meeting.

As years passed on the independent spirit of the times became averse to gagging, though whipping and imprisonment still were for some years dealt out for reviling and railing. America was in some ways earlier in humane elements of consideration for criminals than England, and while women were still wearing the brank in English villages American women no longer feared either gag or cleft stick for unruly tongues.

Long after the punishment of which I write had been banished from American courts it lingered in various forms in American schools — as did the stocks, the penance-stool, and the whip. I have an example of a "whispering-stick," a wooden gag, provided with holes by which it could be tied in place, and which was used in a Providence school during this century as a punishment for whispering. And many a child during the past century had a cleft stick placed on his tongue for ill words or untimely words in school. Sometimes, with an exaggeration of ridicule, a small branch of a tree in full leaf was split and pinched on the tongue — a true pedagogical torture.

IX

PUBLIC PENANCE

The custom of performing penance in public by humiliation in church either through significant action, position or confession has often been held to be peculiar to the Presbyterian and Puritan churches. It is, in fact, as old as the Church of Rome, and was a custom of the Church of England long before it became part of the Dissenters' discipline. All ranks and conditions of men shared in this humiliation. An English king, Henry II, a German emperor, Henry IV, the famous Duchess of Gloucester, and Jane Shore are noted examples; humbler victims for minor sins or offenses against religious usages suffered in like manner. In Scotland the ordeals of sitting on the repentance-stool or cutty-stool were most frequent. In economic and social histories of Scotland, and especially in Edgar's *Old Church Life in Scotland*, many instances are enumerated. Sometimes

Public Penance

the offender wore a repentance-gown of sack-cloth; more frequently he stood or sat bare-foot and barelegged.

In our own day penance has been done in the Scottish Church. In 1876 a woman in Ross-shire sat on the cutty-stool through the whole service with a black shawl over her head; while in February, 1884, one of the ringleaders in the Sabbatarian riots was set on the cutty-stool in Lochcarron church and rebuked for a moral offense which could not, according to the discipline of the Free Church in the Highlands, be fully punished in any other way.

In English churches similar penance was done. In the *History of Wakefield Cathedral* are given the old church-wardens' accounts. In them are many items of the loan of sheets for men and women " to do penance in." About sixpence was the usual charge. For immorality, cheating, defamation of character, disregard of the Sabbath and other transgressions penance was performed. In 1766 penance was thus rendered in Stokesby Church for three Sundays by James Bead-well :

"In the time of Divine service, between the hours of ten and eleven in the forenoon of the same day, in the presence of the whole congregation there assembled, being barehead, barefoot and barelegged, having a white sheet wrapped about him from the shoulder to the feet and a white wand in his hand, where immediately after the reading of the Gospel, he shall stand upon some form or seat before the pulpit or place where the minister readeth prayers and say after him as forthwith, etc."

Clergymen even, if offenders against the established church, were not spared public humiliation. In the year 1534 the vicar of a church in Hull, England, preached a sermon in Holy Trinity church advocating the teaching of the Reformers in Antwerp. He was promptly tried for heresy and convicted. He recanted; and in penance walked around the church on Sunday clad only in his shirt, barefooted and carrying a large faggot in his hand. On the market day he walked around the market-place clad in a similar manner. This really solemn act is robbed of its dignity because of the apparel of the penitent.

A man's shirt is an absurd garment; had the offender been wrapped in a sheet, or robed in sackcloth and ashes, he would been a noble figure, but you cannot grace or dignify a shirt.

With a mingling of barbarity and Christianity unrivalled by any other code of laws issued in America, the *Articles, Lawes, and Orders Divine, Politique and Martiall for the colony of Virginea,* as issued by Sir Thomas Dale, punished offenders against the church and God's word equally by physical and moral penance.

"Noe man shall vnworthilie demeane himselfe vnto any Preacher, or Minister of God's Holy Word, but generally hold them in all reverent regard and dutiful intreatie, otherwise he the offender shall openly be whipt three times, and ask publick forgiveness in the assembly of the congregation three several Saboth daies."

"There is no one man or woman in this Colonie now present, or hereafter to arrive, but shall give vp an account of his and their faith and religion, and repaire vnto the Minister, that by his conference with them, hee may vnderstand, and gather, whether heretofore they have been sufficiently instructed and catechised in the principles and grounds on Religion, whose weaknesse and ignorance herein, the Minister, finding, and advising them in all love and charitie to repair often vnto him to receive therein a greater measure of knowledge, if they shal refuse so to repaire vnto him, and he the Minister give notice thereof vnto the Governour, he shall cause the offender first time of refusall to be whipt, for the second time to be whipt twice, and to acknowledge his fault vpon the Saboth day, in the assembly, and for the third time to be whipt every day vntil he hath made the same acknowledgement, and asked forgivenesse for the same, and shall repaire vnto the Minister, to be further instructed as aforesaid; and vpon the Saboth when the Minister shall catechize and of him demaund any question concerning his faith and knowledge, he shall not refuse to make answer vpon the same perill."

Those who were found to " calumniate, detract, slander, murmur, mutinie, resist, disobey, or neglect" the officers' commands also were to be whipped and ask forgiveness at the Sabbath service. The Puritans were said dreadfully to seek God; far greater must have been the dread of Virginia church folk; and in view of this severity it is not to be wondered that this law had to be issued as a pendant:

"No man or woman, vpon paine of death, shall rune away from the Colonie, to Powhathan or any savage Weroance else whatever."

Bishop Meade, in his history of the Virginia church, tells of offenders who stood in church wrapped in white sheets with white wands in their hands; and other examples of public penance in the Southern colonies are known.

In 1639 Robert Sweet of Jamestown — "a gentleman" — appeared, wrapped in a white sheet, and did penance in church. In Lower Norfolk County, a white man and a black woman stood up together, dressed in white sheets and holding white wands in their hands.

The custom of public confession of sin prevailed in the first Salem church, and thereafter lasted in New England, in modified form for two centuries. Biblical authority for this custom was claimed to rest in certain verses of the eighteenth chapter of the gospel by St. Matthew.

Mr. Charles Francis Adams, in his paper entitled *Some Phases of Morality and Church Discipline in New England*, gives many examples of public confession of sin and public reprimand in the Braintree meeting-house. Manuscript church records which I have examined afford scores, almost hundreds of other examples.

In earliest times, in New England as in Virginia a white robe or white sheet was worn by the offender.

In 1681 two Salem women, wrapped in white, were set on stools " in the middle alley" of the meeting-house through the long service ; having on their heads a paper bearing the name of their crime. In 1659 William Trotter of Newbury, Massachusetts, for his slanderous speeches was enjoined to make " publick acknowledgement " in the church on a lecture-day. On the 20th of September, 1667, Ellinor Bonythorne of

York, Maine, was sentenced "to stand 3 Sabbath dayes in a white sheet in the meeting-house." Another Maine woman, Ruth, the wife of John Gouch, being found guilty of a hateful crime was ordered "to stand in a white sheet publickly in the Congregation at Agamenticus two several Sabbath days, and likewise one day in the General Court."

These scenes were not always productive of true penitence. This affair happened in the Braintree church in 1697, and many others might be cited.

"Isaac Theer was called forth in public, moved pathetically to acknowledge his sin and publish his repentance, who came down and stood against the lower end of the fore seat after he had been prevented by our shutting the east door from going out. Stood impudently and said indeed he owned the sin of stealing and was heartily sorry for it, begged pardon of God and men, and hoped he should do so no more, which was all he would be brought unto, saying his sin was already known; all with a remisse voice so few could hear him. The Church gave their judgment against him that he was a notorious scandalous sinner, and obstinately impenitent. And when I was proceeding to spread before him his sin and wickedness, he, as tis probable, guessing what was like to follow, turned about to goe out, and being desired and charged to tarry and know what the church had to say, he flung out of doors with an insolent manner though silent."

A most graphic description of one of these scenes of public abasement and abnegation is given by Governor John Winthrop in his *History of New England.* The offender, Captain John Underhill, was a brave though blustering soldier, a man of influence throughout New England, a so-called gentleman. And I doubt not that Boston folk tried hard to overlook his transgressions because, " soldiers has their ways." Winthrop wrote thus:

" Captain Underhill being brought by the blessing of God in this church's censure of excommunication to remorse for his foul sins, obtained by means of the elders and others of the church of Boston, a safe conduct under the hand of the governor and one of the council to repair to the church. He came at the

time of the court of assistants, and upon the
lecture day, after sermon, the pastor called
him forth and declared the occasion, and then
gave him leave to speak; and, indeed, it was
a spectacle which caused many weeping eyes,
though it afforded matter of much rejoicing
to behold the power of the Lord Jesus in his
ordinances, when they are dispensed in his
own way, holding forth the authority of his
regal sceptre in the simplicity of the gospel.
He came in his worst clothes, being accus-
tomed to take great pride in his bravery and
neatness, without a band, in a foul linen
cap pulled close to his eyes, and standing
upon a form, he did, with many deep sighs
and abundance of tears, lay open his wicked
course, his adultery, his hypocrisy, his perse-
cution of God's people here, and especially
his pride, as the root of all which caused God
to give him over to his sinful courses, and
contempt of magistrates. * * * * *
He spake well, save that his blubbering,
etc., interrupted him, and all along he discovered a broken and melting heart and gave
good exhortations to take heed of such vani-
ties and beginnings of evil as had occasioned

his fall. And in the end he earnestly and humbly besought the church to have compassion on him and to deliver him out of the hands of Satan."

In truth, the Captain " did protest too much." This well-acted and well-costumed piece of vainglorious repentance was not his first appearance in the Boston meeting-house in this role. Twice before had he been the chief actor in a similar scene, and twice had he been forgiven by the church and by individuals specially injured. He was not alone in his " blubbering," as Winthrop plainly puts it. The minister at Jedburgh, Scotland, for similar offenses, " prostrated himself on the floor of the Assembly, and with weeping and howling, entreated for pardon." He was thus sentenced :

" That in Edinburgh as the capital, in Dundee as his native town, in Jedburgh as the scene of his ministration, he should stand in sack-cloth at the church door, also on the repentance-stool, and for two Sundays in each place."

The most striking and noble figure to suffer

public penance in American history was
Judge Samuel Sewall. He was one of the
board of magistrates who sat in judgment at
the famous witchcraft trials in Salem and
Boston in the first century of New England
life. Through his superstition and by his
sentence, many innocent lives were sacrificed.
Judge Sewall was a steadfast Christian, a
man deeply introspective, absolutely upright,
and painfully conscientious. As years passed
by, and all superstitious excitement was dead,
many of the so-called victims confessed their
fraud, and in the light of these confessions,
and with calmer judgment, and years of un-
shrinking thought, Judge Sewall became con-
vinced that his decisions had been unjust, his
condemnation cruel, and his sentences appall-
ingly awful. Though his public confession
and recantation was bitterly opposed by his
fellow judge, Stoughton, he sent to his minister a written confession of his misjudgment,
his remorse, his sorrow. It was read aloud
at the Sabbath service in the Boston church
while the white-haired Judge stood in the
face of the whole congregation with bowed

head and aching heart. For his self-abnega-
tion he has been honored in story and verse;
honored more in his time of penance than in
the many positions of trust and dignity bestowed on him by his fellow-citizens.

X

MILITARY PUNISHMENTS

An English writer of the seventeenth century, one Gittins, says with a burst of noble and eloquent sentiment: "A soldier should fear only God and Dishonour." Writing with candor he might have added, "but the English soldier fears only his officers." The shocking and frequent cruelty practiced in the English army is now a thing of the past, though it lasted to our own day in the form of bitter and protracted floggings. It is useless to describe one of these military floggings, and superfluous as well, when an absolutely classic description, such as Somerville's, in his *Autobiography of a Workingman*, can be read by all. He writes with stinging, burning words of the punishment of a hundred lashes which he received during his service in the British army, and his graphic sentences cut like the " cat " — we seem to see in lurid outlines the silent, motionless, glittering regiment drawn up in a square four rows deep; the unmoved and indifferent officers, all men of gentle birth and liberal education, but brutalized and inhuman, standing within these lines and near the cruel stake; the impassive quartermaster marking with leisurely and unmoved exactness every powerful, agonizing lash of the bloody whip as it descended on the bare back of a brave British soldier, without one sign of protest or scarce of interest from any of the hundreds who viewed the scene, save on the part of the surgeon, who stood perfunctorily near with basin and drugs to revive the sufferer if he fainted, or stop the punishment if it seemed to foretell a fatal result. We read that raw recruits sometimes cried out or dropped down in the ranks from fright at the first horrifying sight of an army-flogging, but they soon grew scarcely to heed the ever-frequent and brutalizing sight. These floggings were never of any value as a restraint or warning in the army; the whipped and flayed soldiers were ruined in temper and character just as they were often ruined in health. Deaths from exhaustion and mortification from the wounds of the lash were far from infrequent. The story of the inquiry in army circles that led to the disuse of the whip in the British army (as for instance, the *Evidence on Military Punishment* contains some of the most revolting pages ever put in print.

English army-laws of course ruled the royal troops in the American provinces, and the local train bands, and were continued among the volunteer American soldiers of the Revolution. I have read scores of order-books and seen hundreds of sentences to flogging, both during the French and Indian wars, and in the Revolutionary war. A few instances may be given. Edward Munro, of Lexington, Mass., was a Lieutenant in a company of Rangers in 1758, and in 1762 he was Lieutenant in Saltonstall's regiment at Crown Point, and he acted as adjutant for four regiments. His order-book still exists. On October 19, 1762, a court-martial found several soldiers guilty of neglect of duty, and he records that they were sentenced to receive punishment in the following manner:

" Robert McKnight to receive 800 lashes on his naked back with cat-o'-nine-tails. John Cobby to receive 600 lashes in the same manner ; and Peter McAllister 300 lashes in the same maner. The adjutant will see the sentences put in execution by the Drum of the line at 5 o'clock this evening ; the Surgeon to attend the execution."

As Peter McAlister was very young his lashes were remitted. He was led in disgrace to watch the others as they were whipped, two hundred lashes at a time, at the head of the four regiments, *if the surgeon found they could endure it.*

These sentences were horribly severe. Thirty-nine lashes were deemed a cruel punishment. Ten was the more freqent number. Dr. Rea, in his diary, kept before " Ticonderogue," tells of a thousand lashes being given in one case. Another journal tells of fifteen hundred lashes. He also states that he never witnessed a military flogging, as he " found the shreaks and crys satisfactory without the sight." Occasionally a faint gleam of humanity seems dawning, as when we find Colonel Crafts in camp before Boston in 1779 sending out this regimental order:

" The Colonel is extreamly sorry and it gives him pain to think he is at last Obliged to Consent to the Corporal Punishment of one of his regiment. Punishments are extreamly erksome and disagreeable to him but he finds they are unfortunately necessary."

After that date the " cat " was seldom idle in his regiment, as in others in the Continental army. Lashes on the naked back with the cat-o'-nine-tails was the usual sentence, diversified by an occasional order for whipping " with a Burch Rodd on the Naked Breech," or "over such Parts as the commanding officer may apoint." There was, says one diary writer of Revolutionary times, " no spairing of the whip " in the Continental army ; and floggings were given for comparatively trivial offenses such as " wearing a hat uncockt," " malingering," swearing, having a dirty gun, uttering " scurulous " words, being short of ammunition, etc.

A New York soldier in 1676 was accused of pilfering. This was the sentence decreed to him:

"The Court Marshall doth adjudge that the said Melchoir Classen shall run the Gantlope once, the length of the fort: where according to the custom of that punishment, the souldiers shall have switches delivered to them, with which they shall strike him as he passes between them stript to the waist, and at the Fort-gate the Marshall is to receive him, and there to kick him out of the garrison as a cashiered person, when he is no more to returne, and if any pay is due him it is to be forfeited."

All of which would seem to tend to the complete annihilation of Melchoir Classen.

Gantlope was the earlier and more correct form of the word now commonly called gantlet. Running the gantlope was a military punishment in universal use in the seventeenth century in England and on the continent. It was the German *Gassenlaufen* and it is said was the invention of that military genius, the Emperor Gustavus Adolphus.

The method of punishing by running the gantlope was very exactly defined in English martial law. The entire regiment was drawn up six deep. The ranks then were opened and faced inward; thus an open passage way was formed with three rows of soldiers on either side. Each soldier was given a lash or a switch and ordered to strike with force. The offender, stripped naked to the waist, was made to run between the lines, and he was preceded by a sergeant who pressed the point of his reversed halbert against the breast of the unfortunate culprit to prevent his running too swiftly between the strokes. Thus every soldier was made a public executioner of a cowardly and degrading punishment.

Several cases are on record of running the gantlope in Virginia; and an interesting case was that of Captain Walter Gendal of Yarmouth, Maine, a brave soldier, who for the slightest evidence of a not very serious crime was sentenced to "run the gauntelope" through all the military companies in Boston with a rope around his neck. This sentence was never executed.

It is certainly curious to note that the first two parsons who came to Plymouth, named Oldham and Lyford, came in honor and affection, but had to run the gantlope at their leaving. They were most "unsavorie salt," as poor, worried Bradford calls them in his narrative of their misbehaviors (one of the shrewdest, most humorous and sententious pieces of seventeenth century writing extant), and after various " skandales, aggravations, and great malignancies " they were "clapt up for a while." He then writes of Oldham:

"They comited him till he was tamer, and then apointed a guard of musketiers, wch he was to pass thorow, and every man was ordered to give him a thump on ye breech wth ye end of his musket, then they bid him goe and mende his manners."

Morton of Merry-mount tells in equally forcible language in his *New England Canaan* of the similar punishment of Lyford.

A Dutch sailor, for drawing a knife on a companion, was dropped three times from the yard-arm and received a kick from every sailor on the ship — a form of running the gantlope. And we read of a woman who enlisted as a seaman, and whose sex was detected, being dropped three times from the yard-arm, running the gantlope, and being tarred and feathered, and that she nearly died

126

from the rough and cruel treatment she received.

Similar in nature to running the gantlope, and equally cowardly and cruel, was "passing the pikes."

In the fierce *Summarie of Marshall Lawes* for the colony of Virginia under Dale, I find constantly appointed the penalty of "passing the pikes:" it was ordered for disobedience, for persistence in quarrelling, for waylaying to wound, etc.

"That Souldier that having a quarrell with an other, shall gather other of his acquaintances, and associates, to make parties, to bandie, brave second, and assist him therein, he and those braves, seconds and assistants shall pass the pikes."

This was not an idle threat, for duelling was discouraged and forbidden by Virginia rulers. In 1652 one Denham of Virginia carried a challenge from his father-in-law to a Mr. Fox. He was tried for complicity in promoting duelling and thus sentenced:

"For bringinge and acknowledgeinge it to be a chalenge, for deliveringe it to a member of ye court during ye court's siting, for his slytinge and lessinge ye offense together with his premptory answers to ye court ye sd Denham to receave six stripes on his bare shoulder with a whip."

Another common punishment for soldiers (usually for rioting or drinking) was the riding the wooden horse. In New Amsterdam the wooden horse stood between Paerel street and the Fort, and was a straight, narrow, horizontal pole, standing twelve feet high. Sometimes the upper edge of the board or pole was acutely sharpened to intensify the cruelty. The soldier was set astride this board, with his hands tied behind his back. Often a heavy weight was tied to each foot, as was jocularly said, "to keep his horse from throwing him." Garret Segersen, a Dutch soldier, for stealing chickens, rode the wooden horse for three days, from two o'clock to close of parade, with a fifty-pound weight tied to each foot, which was a severe punishment. In other cases in New Amsterdam a musket was tied to each foot of the disgraced man. One culprit rode with an empty scabbard in one hand and a pitcher in the other to show his inordinate love for John Barleycorn.

Jan Alleman, a Dutch officer, valorously challenged Jan de Fries, *who was bedridden;* for this cruel and meaningless insult he, too, was sentenced to ride the wooden horse, and was cashiered.

Dutch regiments in New Netherland were frequently drilled and commanded by English officers, and riding the wooden horse was a favorite punishment in the English army; hence perhaps its prevalence in the Dutch regiments.

Grose, in his *Military History of England,* gives a picture of the wooden horse. It shows a narrow-edged board mounted on four legs on rollers and bearing a rudely-shaped head and tail. The ruins of one was still standing in Portsmouth, England, in 1765. He says that its use was abandoned in the English army on account of the permanent injury to the health of the culprit who endured it. At least one death is known in America, in colonial times, on Long Island, from riding the wooden horse. It was, of course, meted out as a punishment in the American provinces both in the royal troops and in the local train bands.

A Maine soldier, one Richard Gibson, in 1670, was "complayned of for his dangerous and churtonous caridge to his commander and mallplying of oaths." He was sentenced to be laid neck and heels together at the head of his company for two hours, or to ride the " Wooden-Hourse " at the head of the company the next training-day at Kittery.

In 1661, a Salem soldier, for some military misdemeanor, was sentenced to " ride the wooden horse," and in Revolutionary days it was a favorite punishment in the Continental army. In the order-book kept by Rev. John Pitman during his military service on the Hudson, are frequent entries of sentences both for soldiers and suspected spies, to "ride the woodin horse," or, as it was sometimes called, " the timber mare." It was probably from the many hours of each sentence a modification of the cruel punishment of the seventeenth century.

It was most interesting to me to find, under the firm signature of our familiar Revolutionary hero, Paul Revere, as " Preseding Officer," the report of a Court-martial upon two Continental soldiers for playing cards on the Sabbath day in September, 1776; and to know that, as expressed by Paul Revere, "the Court are of the Oppinion that Thomas Cleverly ride the Wooden Horse for a Quarter of an hower with a muskett on each foot, and that Caleb Southward Cleans the Streets of the Camp," which shows that the patriot, could temper justice with both tender mercy and tidy prudence.

The wooden horse was employed some times as a civil punishment. Horse thieves were thus fitly punished. In New Haven, in January, 1787, a case happened:

"Last Tuesday one James Brown, a transient person, was brought to the bar of the County Court on a complaint for horse-stealing — being put to plead — plead guilty, and on Thursday received the sentence of the Court, that he shall be confined to the Goal in this County 8 weeks, to be whipped the first Day 15 stripes on the naked Body, and set an hour on the wooden horse, and on the first Monday each following Month be whipped ten stripes and set one hour each time on the wooden horse."

The cruel punishment of "picketing," which was ever the close companion of "riding the wooden horse" in the English army is recorded by Dr. Rea as constantly employed in the colonial forces. In "picketing" the culprit was strung up to a hook by one wrist while the opposite bare heel rested upon a stake or picket, rounded at the point just enough not to pierce the skin. The agony caused by this punishment was great. It could seldom be endured longer than a quarter of an hour at a time. It so frequently disabled soldiers for marching that it was finally abandoned as "inexpedient."

The high honor of inventing and employing the whirlgig as a means of punishment in the army has often been assigned to our Revolutionary hero, General Henry Dearborn, but the fame or infamy is not his. For years it was used in the English army for the petty offenses of soldiers, and especially of camp-followers. It was a cage which was made to revolve at great speed, and the nausea and agony it caused to its unhappy occupant were unspeakable. In the American army it is said lunacy and imbecility often followed excessive punishment in the whirlgig.

Various tiresome or grotesque punishments were employed. Delinquent soldiers in Winthrop's day were sentenced to carry a large number of turfs to the Fort; others were chained to a wheelbarrow. In 1778 among the Continental soldiers as in our Civil War, culprits were chained to a log or clog of wood; this weight often was worn four days. One soldier for stealing cordage was sentenced to "wear a clogg for four days and wear his coat rong side turn'd out." A deserter from the battle of Bunker Hill was tied to a horse's tail, lead around the camp and whipped. Other deserters were set on a horse with face to the horse's tail, and thus led around the camp in derision.

There was one curious punishment in use in the army during our Civil War which, though not, of course, of colonial times, may well be mentioned since it was a revival of a very ancient punishment. It is thus described by the author of a paper written in 1862 and called *A Look at the Federal Army:*

" I was extremely amused to see a rare

specimen of Yankee invention in the shape of an original method of punishment drill. One wretched delinquent was gratuitously framed in oak, his head being thrust through a hole cut in one end of a barrel, the other end of which had been removed, and the poor fellow loafed about in the most disconsolate manner, looking for all the world like a half-hatched chicken."

I have made careful inquiry among officers and soldiers who served in the late war, and I find this instance, which occurred in Virginia, was not exceptional. A lieutenant in the Maine infantry volunteers wrote on July 13, 1863, from Cape Parapet, about two miles above New Orleans:

" We have had some drunkenness but not so much as when we were in other places ; two of my company were drunk, and the next day I had a hole cut in the head of a barrel, and put a placard on each side to tell the bearer that 'I am wearing this for getting drunk,' and with this they marched through the streets of the regiment four hours each. I don't believe they will get drunk again very soon."

The officer who wrote the above adds to-day:

"This punishment was not original with me, as I had read of its being done in the Army of the Potomac, and I asked permission of the colonel to try it, the taking away of a soldier's pay by court-martial having little permanent effect. In those cases one of the men quit drinking, and years afterward thanked me for having cured him of the habit, saying he had never drank a drop of liquor since he wore the barrel-shirt."

Another Union soldier, a member of Company B, Thirteenth Massachusetts Volunteers, writes that while with General Banks at Darnstown, Virginia, he saw a man thus punished who had been found guilty of stealing: With his head in one hole, and his arms in smaller holes on either side of the barrel, placarded "I am a thief," he was under a corporal's guard marched with a drum beating the rogue's march through all the streets of the brigade to which his regiment was attached. Another officer tells me of thus punishing a man who stole liquor. His barrel was ornamented with bottles on either side simulating

epaulets, and was labelled " I stole whiskey."
Many other instances might be given. There
was usually no military authority for these
punishments, but they were simply ordered in
cases which seemed too petty for the formal-
ity of a court-martial.

This " barrel-shirt," which was evidently
so frequently used in our Civil War, was
known as the Drunkard's Cloak, and it was
largely employed in past centuries on the Continent. Sir William Brereton, in his *Travels
in Holland*, 1634, notes its use in Delft ; so
does Pepys in the year 1660. Evelyn writes
in 1641 that in the Senate House in Delft he
saw " a weighty vessel of wood not unlike a
butter churn," which was used to punish
women, who were led about the town in it.
Howard notes its presence in Danish prisons
in 1784 under the name of the " Spanish
Mantle."

The only contemporary account I know
of its being worn in England is in a book
written by Ralph Gardner, printed in 1655,
and entitled *England's Grievance Discovered*,
etc. The author says :

" He affirms he hath seen men drove up

and down the streets, with a great tub or barrel open in the sides, with a hole in one end to put through their heads, and so cover their shoulders and bodies, down to the small of their legs, and then close the same; called the new-fashion cloak, and so make them march to the view of all beholders, and this is their punishment for drunkards and the like."

It is also interesting and suggestive to note that by tradition the Drunkard's Cloak was in use in Cromwell's army; but the steps that led from its use among the Roundheads to its use in the Army of the Potomac are, I fear, forever lost.

XI

BRANDING AND MAIMING.

There is nothing more abhorrent to the general sentiment of humanity to-day than the universal custom of all civilized nations, until the present century, of branding and maiming criminals. In these barbarous methods of degrading criminals the colonists in America followed the customs and copied the laws of the fatherland. Our ancestors were not squeamish. The sight of a man lopped of his ears, or slit of his nostrils, or with a seared brand or great gash in his forehead or cheek could not affect the stout stomachs that cheerfully and eagerly gathered around the bloody whipping-post and the gallows.

Let us recount the welcome of New England Christians to the first Quakers on American soil. In 1656 the vanguard, two women, Ann Austin and Mary Fisher, appeared in Boston, from the Barbadoes. They

Branding.

were promptly imprisoned and speedily sent
back whence they came; and a premonitory
law was passed to punish shipmasters who
presumed to bring over more Quakers.
Others immediately followed, however, and
fierce laws and cruel sentences greeted them;
within four years after that first appearance
scores of Quakers had been stripped naked,
whipped, pilloried, stocked, caged, imprisoned,
laid neck and heels, branded and maimed;
and four had been hanged in Boston by our
Puritan forefathers. I know nothing more
chilling to our present glow of Puritan an-
cestor-worship in New England than the
reading of Quaker George Bishop's account
of *New England Judged by the Spirit of the
Lord*. Page after page of merciless cruelty is
displayed in forcible, simple language. Here
is an account of a Quaker's treatment in
New Haven for worshipping God in his
chosen way:

"The Drum was Beat, the People gather'd, Norton was fetch'd and stripp'd to the
Waste, and set with his Back to the Magistrates, and given in their View Thirty-six
cruel Stripes with a knotted cord, and his

hand made fast in the Stocks where they had set his Body before, and burn'd very deep with a Red-hot Iron with H. for Heresie."

Quaker women were punished with equal ferocity. Bishop says of Mary Clark:

"Her tender Body ye unmercifully tore with twenty stripes of a three-fold-corded-knotted whip; as near as the Hangman could all in one place, fetching his Stroaks with the greatest Strength & Advantage."

The constables of twelve Massachusetts and New Hampshire towns were notified of four "rougue and vagabond Quakers" named Anna Coleman, Mary Tompkins, Alice Andrews and Alice Ambrose.

"You are enjoined to make them fast to the cart-tail & draw them through your several towns, and whip them on their naked backs not exceeding ten stripes in each town, and so convey them from Constable to Constable on your Perill?"

These women were whipped until the blood ran down their shoulders and breasts, and the men of the town of Salisbury rose in righteous wrath and tore them away from the cart and the constables. Quakers were or-

dered never to return after being banished
from any town. In the " Massachusetts
Colonial Records " of the year 1657 read
the penalty for disobediently returning :

" A Quaker if male for the first offense
shall have one of his eares cutt off ; for the
second offense have his other eare cutt off ;
a woman shalbe severely whipt ; for the third
offense they, he or she, shall have their
tongues bored through with a hot iron."

They were also to be branded with the
letter R on the right shoulder. They were
called " blasphemous hereticks " by the magistrates, and any who read books of their
"devilish opinions " were to be punished
with severity. New York and Virginia were
likewise intolerant and cruel to the Quakers,
but were less visited by them than Massachusetts.

In the despotism of early Virginia, under
the Code of Martial Law established by Sir
Thomas Dale, the fierceness of punishment
was appalling ; possibly the arbitrariness was
necessary to control the turbulent community,
but the cruelty shocked Dale's successor,
Governor Yeardly, who proclaimed that the

"cruel laws by which the Ancient Planters
had been governed" should be abolished.
Under the laws proclaimed by Dale, absence
from church was a capital offense. One
man was broken on the wheel, one of the
few instances known in the colonies. Blasphemy was punished by boring the tongue
with a red hot bodkin ; one offender was thus
punished and chained to a tree to die. A
Mr. Barnes of Bermuda Hundred, for uttering detracting words against another Virginia
gentleman, was condemned to have his tongue
bored through with an awl, to pass through a
guard of forty men, and be butted by every
one of them. At the end to be knocked
down and footed out of the fort, which must
have effectively finished Mr. Barnes of Virginia. Yet Dale was an ardent Christian,
beloved by his pastor, who said he was "a
man of great knowledge in divinity and a
good conscience in all things." He is an
interesting figure in Virginia history — a
sturdy watch-dog — tearing and rending with
a cruelty equal to his zeal every offender
against the common-weal.

In Maryland blasphemy was similarly

punished. For the first offense the tongue was to be bored, and a fine paid of twenty pounds. For the second offense the blasphemer was to be stigmatized in the forehead with the letter B and the fine was doubled. For the third offense the penalty was death. Until the reign of Queen Anne the punishment of an English officer for blasphemy was boring the tongue with a hot iron.

A curious punishment for swearing was ordered by the President of the pioneer expedition into Virginia as told by Captain John Smith. The English gallants who came to the colony for adventure or to escape punishment were very tender-handed. They were sent into the woods to cut down trees for clapboard, but their hands soon blistered under the heavy axe helves, and the pain caused them to frequently cry out in great oaths. The President ordered that every oath should be noted, and for each a can of water was poured down the sleeve of the the person who had been guilty of uttering it. In Haddon, Derbyshire, England, is a relic of a similar punishment, an iron hand-

cuff fastened to the woodwork of the ban-
queting hall. A sneak-cup who "balked his
liquor" or any one who committed any vio-
lation of the convivial customs of that day
and place, had his wrist placed in the iron
ring, and a can of cold water, or the liquor
he declined was poured up his sleeve.

It is interesting to note in the statutes of
Virginia and Maryland the honor that for
decades hedged around the domestic hog.
The crime of hog stealing is minutely defined and specified, and vested with bitter
retribution. It was enacted by the Maryland
Assembly that for the first offense the criminal should stand in the pillory " four Com-
pleat hours," have his ears cropped and pay
treble damages; for the second offense be
stigmatized on the forehead with the letter H
and pay treble damages; for the third be adjudged a " fellon," and therefore receive
capital punishment. In Virginia in 1748 the
hog-stealer for the first offense received
"twenty-five lashes well laid on at the publick whipping-post;" for the second offense
he was set two hours in the pillory and had
both ears nailed thereto, at the end of the

two hours *to have the ears slit loose;* for the
third offense, death. Were the culprit in
either province a slave, the cruelty and punishment were doubled. For all hog-stealers,
whether bond or free, there was no benefit of
clergy, which was the ameliorating plea, per-
missible in some felonies of being able to
read " clerkly."

It is evident that in early days this plea
could not extend to a very large number in
any community. It was originally a monkish
privilege extended to English ecclesiastics in
criminal processes in secular courts. It was
granted originally in 1274 and was not abolished in England till 1827. The minutes
of the Court of General Quarter Sessions
in New York bear many records of criminals who pleaded " the benefit," and instead
of hanging on a gallows, were branded on the
brawn of the left thumb with T in open
court and then discharged. Benefit of clergy
existed and was in force in New York state
till February 21, 1788.

In Salem men and women offenders constantly pleaded commutation through benefit of
clergy. In 1750 a counterfeiter of that time

was sentenced to death. He pleaded benefit of clergy, and was respited, and instead of his original sentence was burnt in the hand. A woman for polyandry was similarly benefited by the same plea. This power of claiming amelioration of sentence lasted in Massachusetts till the year 1785, when it was forever nullified by the laws of Massachusetts under the new United States. In Virginia, benefit of clergy was a constant plea, and was recognized in all cases save, as has been said, in hog-stealing.

In Maryland branding was legal, and every county was ordered to have branding-irons. The lettering was specifically defined and enjoined. S. L. stood for seditious libel, and could be burnt on either cheek. M. stood for manslaughter, T. for thief, and could be branded on the left hand. R. was for rogue or vagabond, and was branded on the shoulder. Coiners could for the second offense be branded on the cheek F. for forgery.

Burglary was punished in all the colonies by branding. By the Provincial laws of New Hampshire, of 1679, a burglar was branded with a capital B in the right hand for the first offense, in the left hand for the second, "and if either be committed on the Lord's Daye his Brand shall bee sett on his Forehead." By Governor Eaton's Code of Laws for the Connecticut colonists the punishment was equally severe.

"If any person commit Burglary or rob any person on the Lord's Day he shalbe burned and whipped and for a second offense burned on the left hand, stand in the Pillory and wear a halter around his neck in the daytime visibly as a mark of infamy."

A forger of deeds could be branded in the forehead with the letter F; while for defacing the records the offender could be disfranchised and branded in the face. A forger was branded in Worcester in 1769. A man who sold arms and powder and shot to the Indians was branded with the letter I. Counterfeiters were branded and often had the ears cropped.

A conviction and sentence in Newport in 1771 was thus reported in the daily newspapers:

"William Carlisle was convicted of passing Counterfeit Dollars, and sentenced to stand One Hour in the Pillory on Little-Rest Hill, next Friday, to have both Ears cropped, to be branded on both Cheeks with the Letter R, to pay a fine of One Hundred Dollars and cost of Prosecution, and to stand committed till Sentence performed."

In Virginia many offenses were punished by loss of the ears or by slitting the ears. Among other penalties decreed to " deceiptful bakers," dishonest cooks, cheating fishermen, or careless fish dressers was " to loose his eares."

Truly long hair and wigs had their ulterior uses in colonial days when ear-cropping was thus rife. Romantic old tales of life on the road tell of carefully hidden deformities, of mysterious gauntleted strangers, whose hands displayed when revealed the lurid brand of past villainies. Life was dull and cramped in those days, but there were diversions; when the breeze might lift the locks from your friends or your lover's cheek and give a glimpse of ghastly hole instead of an ear, or display a burning letter on the forehead; when his shoulder under his lace collar might be branded with a rogue's mark, or be banded beneath his velvet doublet with the scars and welts of fierce lashes of the cat-o'-nine tails.

Brand and brank have passed away, the stocks and pillory no longer grace our village greens. We pride ourselves on our humanity, our justice. Therefore it may be well to note that we have now in the United States the most extreme code in the entire world in regard to capital punishment—sixty-two crimes punishable by death. A bill is before the Senate to strike sixteen offenses from our brutal list. Belgium, Holland, Brazil, Italy, Portugal, Gautemala, Venezuela and Costa Rica have wholly abolished the death penalty. In cruel Russia the death sentence has been since 1753 never pronounced save for treason, while China has only eleven capital offenses. We have adhered to obsolete English laws while England has done away with them and has now only four capital crimes. It is certainly surprising and even mortifying to know that in Maryland setting fire to a hay-rick is to this day punishable by death.